CASE STUDIES IN
CULTURAL ANTHROPOLOGY

GENERAL EDITORS
George and Louise Spindler
STANFORD UNIVERSITY

---

BENABARRE:

*The Modernization of a Spanish Village*

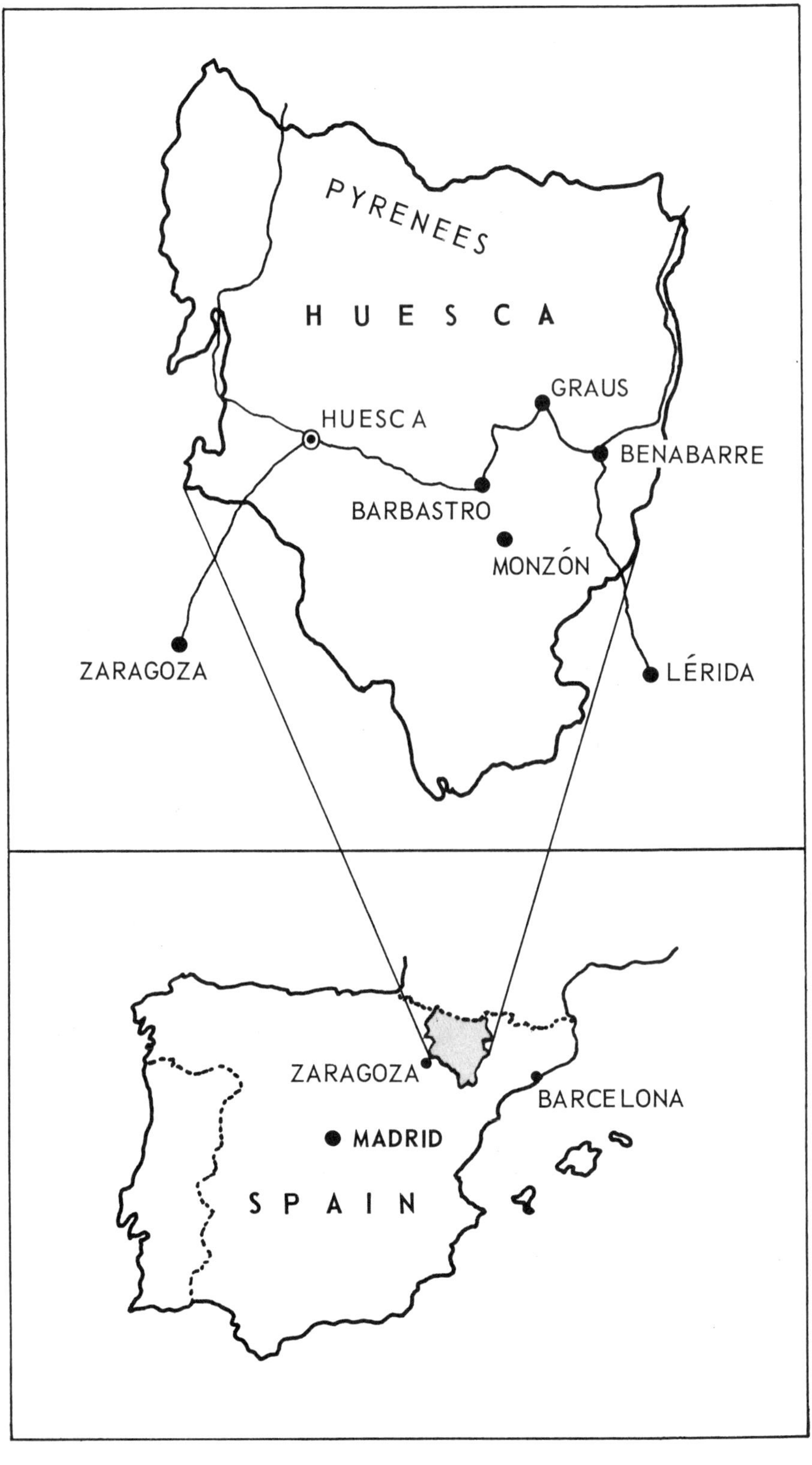
PYRENEES
HUESCA
GRAUS
HUESCA
BENABARRE
BARBASTRO
MONZÓN
ZARAGOZA
LÉRIDA
ZARAGOZA
BARCELONA
MADRID
SPAIN

# BENABARRE:
# THE MODERNIZATION OF
# A SPANISH VILLAGE

By
RICHARD A. BARRETT
*University of New Mexico*

HOLT, RINEHART AND WINSTON, INC.
NEW YORK   CHICAGO   SAN FRANCISCO   ATLANTA
DALLAS   MONTREAL   TORONTO   LONDON   SYDNEY

Library of Congress Cataloging in Publication Data

Barrett, Richard A.
Benabarre: the modernization of a Spanish village.

(Case studies in cultural anthropology)
Bibliography: p. 107
1. Benabarre, Spain—Social conditions.
2. Benabarre, Spain—Politics and government.
3. Benabarre, Spain—Economic conditions. I. Series.
HN590.B47B37     309.1′46′555     73-17424
ISBN 0-03-008201-3

Copyright © 1974 by Holt, Rinehart and Winston, Inc.
All rights reserved
Printed in the United States of America
3 4 5 6 7   059   9 8 7 6 5 4 3 2 1

*To Yuki*

# Foreword

### ABOUT THE SERIES

These case studies in cultural anthropology are designed to bring to students, in beginning and intermediate courses in the social sciences, insights into the richness and complexity of human life as it is lived in different ways and in different places. They are written by men and women who have lived in the societies they write about and who are professionally trained as observers and interpreters of human behavior. The authors are also teachers, and in writing their books they have kept the students who will read them foremost in their minds. It is our belief that when an understanding of ways of life very different from one's own is gained, abstractions and generalizations about social structure, cultural values, subsistence techniques, and the other universal categories of human social behavior become meaningful.

### ABOUT THE AUTHOR

Richard A. Barrett received his training in anthropology at the University of California at Los Angeles and at the University of Michigan, earning his doctorate at the latter school in 1970. He has taught at Temple University and is presently Assistant Professor of Anthropology at the University of New Mexico. His acquaintance with Spanish culture antedates the period of fieldwork upon which this book is based. In 1960-1961, while still an undergraduate, he lived for a year in Spain and studied at the University of Madrid. His research interests center on problems of modernization in Latin America and in the Mediterranean area. He hopes to return to Spain in the near future to conduct research in a Spanish city.

### ABOUT THE BOOK

On one of our recent trips through Spain we detoured especially to visit Benabarre, since we had already been introduced to the village by a preliminary manuscript from Richard Barrett. Noting the impressive castle and the hilly environs of Benabarre from a distance, we proceeded on a small road through the lower part of the village and wound our way up to an area where there were several pleasant villas along one side of the road and the community water supply on the other. We wanted to eat our lunch and contemplate the lay of the village, as well as take a few pictures, before reconnoitering the community itself. As we got out of our car, two men, who had apparently been working on the water system, came walking towards us and we engaged them in conversation. After some preliminaries, we asked if they had known a young man who had done a sociological study of Benabarre a short time ago. Their faces lit up and they spoke of their friend, Richard Barrett, with great enthusiasm and warmth. He was "*muy simpático.*" They told us a good deal about him, about his Japanese wife, and his participation in the life of Benabarre. Our inadequate Spanish permitted us to catch only a portion of what was said, but it was very clear that they felt most warmly about their friend, Barrett, and that he had acted as a good anthropologist should. They took special delight in telling us about how he could sit at a cafe all afternoon with only a little bit of wine (indicating with two fingers the miniscule quantity) talking to everyone. "He knew everyone and talked to them about everything." They then referred us to a Señor Tomás "who knows everything you would be interested in." We spent an interesting day in Benabarre.

That our two informants had good reason to speak of Richard Barrett as they did becomes apparent as one reads through the first part of this case study, which is devoted to how the anthropologist learned about Benabarre and how the Benabarrenses came to know him. In this part of the case study he introduces us to the community and the people in it as well as acquainting us with his procedures of fieldwork and his rationale for them. He makes the interesting point that the anthropologist must come to know the culture of the community not only as the natives know it but also in a way that they do not know it. This is a very obvious fact, but one that is often overlooked in contemporary discussions of the relationship of the anthropologist to the community he studies and to the people who live in it.

This case study documents the effects of modernization and urbanization upon the small community in a particularly significant context. During the last two decades Spain has achieved levels of growth greater than at any other period of its history and exhibits one of the highest rates of development in the western world. These generalizations have specific meaning in Benabarre and the author develops this meaning explicitly. Urbanization in Spain has occurred at the cost of a rural exodus that has virtually depopulated the countryside in certain areas. The hinterland around Benabarre has lost 61 percent of its population in twenty years. Many small and relatively isolated communities are now completely abandoned with boarded-up windows, utter silence, and collapsing roofs. Even Benabarre has lost 45 percent of its population between 1910 and 1970. This shift in population has been due both to a breakdown in the traditional economy and to an increase in opportunities in urban centers. Even these dramatic figures do not tell the whole story. Many households, apparently still intact, will not survive for another generation for the young people will not suffer the relative deprivation associated with small scale farming or other traditional enterprises, and local girls become increasingly reluctant to marry into peasant households.

There are many parallels here to processes of change described in the studies of Burgbach and Kippel in this same series.* In both cases it is the smallhold

---

\* George D. Spindler and student collaborators, 1973, *Burgbach: Urbanization and Identity in a German Village,* Case Study in Cultural Anthropology. New York: Holt, Rinehart and Winston, Inc.

John Friedl, 1974, *Kippel: A Changing Village in the Alps,* Case Study in Cultural Anthropology. New York: Holt, Rinehart and Winston, Inc.

peasant, whose landholdings are fragmented and whose methods of operation are traditional, who is losing out. Mechanization is effective only on consolidated and larger landholdings. Farming as a way of life is displaced by farming as a rationalized industry. This change strikes directly at the core of the traditional folk culture.

In all three cases, however, modernization not only results in the loss of the traditional way of life and a disorganization of traditional patterns, but also results in regenerative and creative processes. The area around Benabarre is becoming a rural food factory with a number of mass production units developing in livestock, poultry, and egg farming. Construction work has increased as urbanites buy and renovate old buildings, or build new summer homes. Tourism is taking on economic significance, and many people now derive income from apartment rentals. Property values have also increased. The character of life and interpersonal relations and the class structure itself are undergoing fundamental change. Benabarre, of course, is different from Burgbach because the latter is becoming incorporated into a larger metropolitan whole. A more total kind of urbanization is taking place there. In Benabarre and Kippel, due to their relative remoteness from urban centers, the process is less complete. Both Benabarre and Kippel have retained their identities, though they have become much more open to outside influences and personnel in recent decades. These case studies, read singly or together, will give the student an understanding of the processes of urbanization and modernization, as they apply to small communities, that no amount of generalizing could.

GEORGE AND LOUISE SPINDLER<br>
*General Editors*

Portola Valley, California

# Acknowledgments

Fieldwork in Benabarre in 1967-1968 was supported by a fellowship from the "project for the study of social networks in the Mediterranean area" which was financed by a grant from the Ford Foundation. I am grateful to the project directors Eric R. Wolf and William D. Schorger for the fellowship. I also had support while preparing for fieldwork from a predoctoral fellowship (No. 5-F1-MA-30, 519-02) from the National Institutes of Mental Health.

In writing this book I have incurred numerous debts. Eric Wolf was a constant source of advice and inspiration, both while I was in the field and afterwards when I wrote my doctoral dissertation. Anybody familiar with his work will recognize his influence in the treatment of materials here. Some years ago Charles Gibson also gave me some good advice which I have taken to heart in writing this account. My colleague Philip Bock read three chapters of this manuscript and made some very useful suggestions, and I thank him. George and Louise Spindler, the editors of this series, have also given help and encouragement. I thank Charla Schwerstein for typing the manuscript.

There are various persons in Spain who gave very generously of their time. I want to particularly thank my good friends in Benabarre. The good people of La Buena de Dios, Casa Escolá, Casa Rodrigo Rico, Casa Isidro, Casa Fort and of the Mas de Pinies—all were of enormous help to me. There are many others in the village whom I can only thank collectively. I benefited greatly from the knowledge of Don Francisco Abbad, one of the most engaging and erudite individuals I have ever had the pleasure to meet. Don Marcelino Mur-Saludas, a former *secretario* of Benabarre, was kind enough to share his thoughts about Benabarre with me, and I thank him.

Perhaps my greatest debt is to my wife Yukiko. She listens, sometimes patiently, to my ideas before they are shared with the rest of the world. Unlike other critics, she has no reserve in expressing disapproval.

R. A. B.

# Contents

Foreword     vii

Acknowledgments     xi

1. The Setting and Fieldwork     1

    *The Setting*   1
    *Fieldwork*   4
      Establishing Rapport   5
      Use of Informants   10
      Participant Observation   17

2. The Background: Prewar Society     23

    *The Class Division in the Prewar Community*   23
    *The Gentleman Complex*   26
    *Interclass Relations*   30
    *The Notables as "Brokers"*   35
    *The Second Republic and Civil War*   36

3. Benabarre in the Rural Revolution     39

    *Industrial Development in Spain*   39
    *The Rural Exodus*   41
    *The Crisis of the Small Proprietor*   44
    *Metropolitan Culture and the Urban Impulse*   51
    *The New Economy*   55

4. The Changing Class Structure     60

    *Social Leveling*   60
    *The Rural Bourgeoisie*   64
    *Social Withdrawal of the Notables*   66
    *The New Middle Class*   69
    *The Traditional Farmers*   74
    *The Skilled Trades*   76

5. The Village and the Outside World     78

    *City-Village Social Ties*   78
    *Urban-Rural Reciprocity*   81
    *Extra-Community Networks: Political Implications*   85

xiv   CONTENTS

    *Influential Hijos del Pueblo* 90
    *Institutions and Networks* 92
    *The Character of Village Government* 95

6. Conclusions: Balance Sheet on Modernization    98

    *Loss of Community* 98
    *The Economic and Political Dimension* 103
    *Final Remarks* 105

References Cited    107

Recommended Reading    109

# BENABARRE

# 1 / The setting and fieldwork

The cultural anthropologist typically studies small, face-to-face communities. By immersing himself as deeply as he can in local life he gains an intimate familiarity with the people and the way of life he studies. What he sacrifices in scope he hopes to attain in immediacy of knowledge. Few anthropologists would, however, concede that the relevance of their studies is confined to the immediate communities dealt with. The anthropologist who writes about a village in India also expects to add to our knowledge of Indian culture; the one who writes about American street-corner blacks aims at making some statement about the black situation in the United States.

It is likewise with this study. I am concerned with a small village in northern Spain. Without saying that the village is typical of community life—for in many ways it is not—I do think that it reflects a great deal of Spanish culture. More importantly, the community is representative of a change which is occurring throughout the Spanish countryside and elsewhere in the world. Spain is experiencing what one anthropologist has termed the "rural revolution" (Halpern 1967). This is the change initiated in agrarian countries when these nations begin to make successful strides toward industrialization. Since the 1950s Spain has been making rapid progress toward this goal and the impact on the villages has been considerable. The rural revolution is by no means confined to Spain. Many other countries, of southern Europe, the Middle East, Latin America, and Asia, are undergoing a similar transformation. Detailed studies can provide important insights into the course of change in developing countries. A principal aim of this study is to point up some of the social and political changes which accompany, or are a consequence of, industrial modernization. Of course in many ways the Spanish case is unique, as any historical experience must be. Nevertheless, it is unique within a series of events which exhibit similarities. Hopefully, case studies such as this one will aid us in understanding the regularities in the process of modernization as a whole.

## THE SETTING

The village of Benabarre is located in Huesca province in the northeastern part of Spain. It is situated in the northern half of the province in a broad belt of foothills and low mountains referred to as the sub-Pyrenean zone. The elevation of

*The village is built on a hill which is crowned by the castle of the* Condes de Ribagorza.

the village plaza is 2,350 feet above sea level. The intermediate elevation gives the area a rather mild climate. The winters are cold but not severely so; snow falls on only a few days each year and it typically melts after a few hours on the ground. In summer the climate is almost ideal; the average midday temperatures range, from late June to August, between 68 and 80 degrees Fahrenheit. The cool, pleasant summers make Benabarre an attractive resort for summer visitors from the lowland cities.

Apart from a pleasant climate, Benabarre also has a certain aesthetic charm—at least from the point of view of foreign or outside visitors. The village is perched on a rocky hill and crowned by a medieval castle. As the castle suggests, the community dates far back in history; nobody is certain how far. The village is mentioned in historical records as early as the tenth century when the region as a whole was contested between Christians and Moors. It was obviously a fortified site in the Middle Ages and the castle was its defensive position. We know that the castle was used for defense as late as the Carlist wars of the last century. The hillside village and castle make Benabarre an especially impressive sight when seen

[1] The importance of the castle as a scenic landmark is in sharp contrast to the attitude of villagers toward it. Except for children, Benabarrenses do not visit the castle; they are indifferent to its history, and are either puzzled or mildly amused that tourists find it of any interest. One enterprising villager even uses it as a pen for goats and chickens. When I mentioned this to one of my informants he merely shrugged and said, "Well, it [the castle] might as well be used for something."

from a distance.[1] Internally, the village also has a certain charm. The main road leads to a tree-lined central plaza which gives off to a number of lanes which wind throughout the community. Houses are built in apartment fashion, attached to each other along the streets. The solid rows of buildings give the streets an almost tunnel-like appearance.

Benabarre's population was 1,127 persons in 1968. Most of these (976 persons) live in the village nucleus. There are sixty-six more who live on thirteen farms scattered throughout the village *término* (boundary). Another eighty-five inhabit the small hamlet of Aler which is located five kilometers to the west, but which belongs to Benabarre administratively. There is only one town in the surrounding area larger than Benabarre; this is Graus, 20 kilometers to the northwest, with 3,800 inhabitants. The closest cities are Barbastro, 52 kilometers to the southwest, and Lérida, 65 kilometers directly south. While it is evident that Benabarre is considerable distance from these cities, this should not give the impression that it is isolated. Two asphalt highways meet in Benabarre and connect it to all of the important cities of the plain below. Virtually every day of the year some Benabarrenses visit Lérida, Barbastro, or Huesca, either by bus, taxi, or private car.

The village economy is divided between agriculture and commerce. Like all villages of the region, Benabarre is surrounded by fragmented plots of farmland cultivated by peasants who reside in the village. Each day they drive their tractors, or walk their mules, to their individual holdings and then return to the village in the evening. The agriculture is Mediterranean dry farming. As the name implies, there is no substantial irrigation and crops are dependent on rainfall. The main crops are wheat, barley, oats, wine grapes, almonds, and olives. Of these, cereals are most important; in 1960, 1,526 of Benabarre's 2,087 cultivated hectares were planted in cereals. This represents 73 percent of the cultivated land. Another 304 hectares are in olive trees, 155 are planted with almonds, and 86 in vineyards. This crop complex is supplemented by raising livestock, especially pigs, poultry, and sheep.

Besides farming, Benabarre has a substantial commercial sector. There are various grocery and drygoods stores, four cafes, various butcher shops, blacksmitheries, and carpentries; there are two main banks, a pharmacy, an inn, hotel, and a cinema. The commercial establishments, however, are not highly visible. The stores often have no signs, or poorly discernible ones, and most operate on a small scale. For these reasons the average observer imagines the village economy to be more agrarian than it is. The fact is, however, that a majority of the household heads, 57.5 percent of them, earn more than half of their income from occupations outside of agriculture. The commercial development is due to the fact that Benabarre serves a hinterland population from peasant hamlets which have almost no merchants. Also in recent years a substantial trade has grown up based on highway traffic which passes through the village in a continuous flow.

There is more to be said in introducing the village and people. Yet a purely descriptive account can provide only a limited impression of what the people and community are like. Perhaps if I describe how I came to know Benabarre, something of the people and the impression they made on me will be revealed.

## FIELDWORK

My wife and I arrived in Barcelona in April 1967. After purchasing a small used car we set out for Huesca province. I went there as a doctoral student in anthropology as part of the "project for the study of social networks in the Mediterranean area," based at the University of Michigan. Various areas of Mediterranean countries had been marked out by the project directors as being of particular interest. One of these was the sub-Pyrenees region of northern Spain. The project directors did not attempt to influence my decisions regarding selection of a community, or in focusing on a particular problem for study; these decisions were left up to me. Though I had spent a year in Spain some seven years earlier (and so spoke Spanish), I had never been in this area of the country. Therefore, the first order of business was to carry out a reconnaissance to decide which community would best suit my purposes.

I was interested in studying social stratification and local political organization, so I wanted a medium sized village where there would be merchants and professional people as well as peasants. The small villages tended to be composed almost entirely of peasants and so provided almost no opportunity of observing the relationships between various social and occupational strata. Once in the provincial capital (the city of Huesca) we made a list of all the towns and villages which had more than 1,000 population. We then mapped out daily reconnaissance routes which would allow us to visit three or four villages every day. A typical visit simply entailed driving into the village plaza, getting out, and walking through the streets to talk to anyone who was disposed to talk with us. Fortunately the appearance of strangers (especially foreigners—and my wife is Japanese, and so *very* foreign) is a great event in most Spanish villages and we immediately became a center of curiosity. We never had difficulty finding people with whom to converse.

From the first day of these visits we became aware of a somewhat distressing fact: a great many villages were in a state of serious decline due to an enormous flow of emigration to the cities. Almost all of them had lost population in recent years and in some the loss was so great the villages were literally falling into ruins. Everywhere we heard the same story: "Young people won't stay in the villages; they all run off to the cities." The truth of this statement was reflected in the low percentage of young and working age population in most of the communities we visited. This became an important factor in our choice of a community. We wanted to avoid working in a moribund village and so crossed all of the seriously stricken ones off our list.

We drove into Benabarre on the third day of our reconnaissance. We were immediately impressed by the level of activity. There were numerous construction projects, new livestock farms, many commercial establishments, and even an area for summer tourist cottages being planned outside the community. And although urban emigration was reducing the population, there was no aura of decline.

For a period of about two weeks we balanced the attractions and disadvantages of a number of communities. After living for five days in another village, we decided to stay for awhile in Benabarre. It was apparent from the first few days that Benabarre fit most of the requirements of my research design, and within our first week we made the decision to stay. Yet it would be less than truthful not to mention that various other factors affected our decision. One consideration was that our reception had been better in Benabarre than anywhere else. From the beginning I met two persons whom I was certain would be good informants and both of them strongly encouraged us to stay. To the person who has not done anthropological fieldwork this may seem like a trivial criterion to influence community selection. Yet the ability to establish good personal relationships is the essence of effective fieldwork. Without the approval, or at least acquiescence, of the people it may be impossible to do any work at all. Not infrequently, anthropologists have found community resistance and noncooperation to be insurmountable obstacles to their plans. In Benabarre we seemed to be over the hurdle of initial acceptance from the beginning. A second factor which encouraged us to decide in favor of Benabarre was that we found excellent living conditions. We were able to rent a modern, three room apartment in the center of the village for about thirty dollars a month. It had butane gas for cooking, warm water, flush toilets, a bath, and more space than we could use. So almost immediately we were able to solve most of the problems of basic living needs and physical comfort.

*Establishing Rapport.* It took us a few days to get settled, after which I was ready to begin systematic work. This was my first fieldwork experience and I was anxious to start collecting the information I had come for. I was soon to find, however, that the community was not nearly as ready as I was. The villagers were wary of people who appeared as if out of the blue and claimed they were going to study the community. Despite the fact that I received some encouraging help in those early days, the average villager had a definite wait-and-see attitude. He might not be against us, but neither was he going to involve himself in something which might lead to complications. I almost certainly made the early period more difficult than it had to be by creating undue suspicion. One mistake was in taking notes publicly in the first few weeks. I simply was not sensitive to how frightening pen and paper could be when people did not know what I was writing down. I also asked certain questions, such as on household economies, which should have been saved until I had established better rapport. At any rate, as I found later, numerous rumors began to fly about what we were up to. The most widespread was that we were communist spies. Another was that we were CIA agents (the Spanish newspapers were full of CIA activities in the Middle East at the time). At least a few people thought we might be Protestant missionaries. And most alarming of all, that we were government agents collecting information for tax purposes. I imagine that these rumors only circulated among a small minority, but the fact that people were able to entertain such notions demonstrates how baffling to them our behavior and activities were. Whenever I was directly asked what our mission was I tried to explain as simply as possible: that an American university had sent me to learn as much as I could about life in this part of Spain and I would eventually write a book about it. I soon learned to avoid calling myself an anthropologist because in Spain the word conjures up notions of physical anthropology, fossil bones and so on. The term *sociólogo* (sociologist) communicated more clearly the kind of work I did.

I began to realize that there was going to be a rather lengthy settling-in period

*Three elderly villagers relax on a summer afternoon.*

and I would have to proceed slowly and patiently. Fortunately there were certain kinds of information, like official records, which did not depend on informants. The village *secretario* (in practice the most important village official) had kindly told me that town hall (*ayuntamiento*) records would be at my disposal. So I began spending every morning for a couple of weeks copying census records, data on landholding, the number of automobiles, trucks, tractors owned by villagers, and a good deal more. The officials in the municipal court were equally helpful in providing data on births, marriages, and deaths over the last decades. In the afternoons I would relax a bit and make myself visible, allowing people to become accustomed to my presence. I would go to the cafes to talk with someone, or spend time with my established friends. Through their introductions I slowly began to widen my circle of acquaintances.

Surprisingly, one of the events which helped speed my integration into the community was the departure of my wife. She had her own studies to pursue in Madrid so was not going to be with me most of the year. Once I was alone in Benabarre I had to make new eating arrangements. I found shopping and preparing my own meals extremely time-consuming, so I began taking my afternoon meal in the house of one of my best informants. Various other people took meals in this house and it became a way station for meeting new people. Also without my wife I found I was treated with less formality. People who had been hesitant to interrupt a family situation now had much less hesitancy about dropping by to see me. I was invited to go with men into the fields, and the veterinary asked me to accompany him almost every day as he went on his rounds to various villages. Then some of the village women felt sorry for me, having to live alone without a woman, and so I was invited for meals with some regularity. The new closeness I felt to villagers undoubtedly also had to do with the fact that the loneliness occasioned by my wife's absence encouraged me to seek new social contacts.

One of the most fortunate things to happen to me in this early period was the friendship offered by one of the village bakers, José Pellicer. José took a deep interest in me and my work, and was clearly anxious to be of service. As a personality he stands out in Benabarre due to his very direct manner and for what might even be called a lack of diplomacy. Most Benabarrenses, especially in dealings with strangers, are exceedingly polite and careful to observe the amenities of proper behavior. José is strikingly less concerned on this account. Almost from our first conversation he used the familiar form of address (*tú*) with me and I gladly reciprocated. Nobody else had yet attempted this kind of familiarity. José understood that I was anxious to meet people and he began taking me to visit the persons he thought were most interesting in and around Benabarre. He had almost a sociologist's flair for intriguing personalities and situations. Every afternoon I would climb on the back of his motor scooter and we would set off. I rarely knew where we were going. One day we would drop in on peasants eating their afternoon meal in the fields; the next day we might visit a remote countryhouse; then he would take me to visit one of the elite families of the region; afterwards we might visit the poorest old widow in Benabarre. No matter who it was, José felt no compunction in dropping in unannounced to present me. It was clear this was unconventional behavior, and more than once I can remember feeling embarrassed and ill at ease. Yet it was through these visits that I first glimpsed a genuine cross section of life in Benabarre and began to get a feel for the range of social differences which existed. Unfortunately our rambles could not continue indefinitely. It turned out that José was virtually deserting his work and family to spend time with me; his wife and children, who had to take up the slack, began to protest vigorously. Our excursions eventually had to be limited to those times, such as Saturday and Sunday afternoons, when José was genuinely free of work.

By completion of my second month in Benabarre I felt I had made a fairly good adjustment. Yet there still seemed to be a kind of barrier I had not penetrated with a sizeable segment of the population. The wariness continued and I occasionally caught fragments of rumors which were to the effect that I was not what I pretended to be. Then an event occurred which brought a rather sudden breakthrough in my relations with villagers. This was the visit to Benabarre of Don Tomás Mur, a college professor from Barcelona. His family is descended from Benabarre and they own a house there to which they return every year for summer vacations. When he was told there was a sociologist in Benabarre he wasted no time in having us introduced. He is a professor of languages, but has deep interest in sociology and politics. Don Tomás, in fact, figures among the most erudite and cultivated gentlemen I have met in my life. He retains a vast store of information on Benabarre's recent history, particularly at the crucial period of the Civil War —which happened to catch him in the village. We spent a number of evenings together, in the central plaza, or walking up and down the streets. He would talk and I wrote down what he said as near to verbatim as possible. Thus almost everybody in Benabarre had a chance to see us together and to see Don Tomás actively aiding my work. Nothing could have had a more beneficial effect on my relations with the community. Don Tomás enjoys immense respect and popularity among the villagers, and the fact that he found my work significant was a behavioral cue for a great many people. The reasoning was apparently that if I were someone to beware of, Don Tomás would not be fooled; if *he* believed I was the genuine article, then I must be! The response was immediate. Doors which until then had been closed to me opened up; new people greeted me on the streets and volunteered their services.

At this point I bcame aware that I had made a rather serious error in interpreting community social relations. I had not appreciated the extent to which Benabarrenses take their behavioral cues hierarchically—that is, from the elites. When I entered Benabarre I had incorrectly assumed that it would be best, at least for the initial period, to avoid close association with the professionals and few families which represented the social upper crust. I thought that if there were polarization between the social strata this might make it more difficult later to win acceptance among the peasants. It was virtually the opposite! The fact that I was *not* associating with those who were considered my peers was simply confusing, and made it vastly more difficult to place me in the social order. Once Don Tomás extended his friendship, and introduced me to other families of similar social rank, this served almost as a certificate of respectability.

I learned other dramatic lessons in that first month or two. I have already mentioned that I made a mistake in public notetaking. One of the real lessons of fieldwork consists of learning the occasions when it is appropriate to write and when it is not. On one of my excursions with José the baker I was taken to meet one of his friends who was working in the vineyards. In a rather garbled introduction I was presented to the man and then the three of us sat in the shade to talk, and drink a bit of wine. The man apparently did not realize that I was a foreigner and treated me as if I were simply one of José's city relatives. The conversation became animated and the two of them began telling Civil War stories. This eventually led José's friend to tell a series of jokes about the present Spanish government. At some point in the conversation I was interested enough to want to jot something down. As I took out a pen and pocket notebook I realized the conversation had suddenly stopped. The man across from me had turned ashen pale and there was a look of genuine terror in his eyes. He apparently thought I was writing down one of his antigovernment remarks. He was visibly shaken and asked José again who I was. The answer, that I was an American here to study the region, seemed to unsettle him even more. From that point forward he seemed afraid to say anything on any subject. José and I took our leave very shortly. When we got back to the scooter José shook his head and said, "You really botched that one!"

This incident made me aware of the very different attitudes toward writing in peasant Spain as compared with those in my own background. For the Spanish peasant, information which is written down suggests officialdom, and because he generally thinks of himself as the victim of official acts, the association is anything but pleasant. From that point on I avoided writing where it might cause alarm. This meant waiting until I knew people well, or until I was certain they were familiar with my work. If this were not the case I would simply make mental notes to be written down later. If there was going to be some time before I could write, I would jot down a few key words of an idea in a pocket notebook. Later these words or phrases were expected to recall the whole concept, so when I got back to the apartment I would be able to write the full version in my permanent fieldnotes.

It is worth mentioning that as fieldwork progressed there was a gradually diminishing need for secrecy. As people became accustomed to the idea that I was writing a book, and that I seemed to seek information almost everywhere, most people wanted to participate. Eventually the incident I have described above was reversed. I remember going to a house at the invitation of a man who said he wanted to talk to me. I had taken a seat in the kitchen and we were exchanging small talk when he abruptly asked where my notebook was. I replied I had not brought it. "But don't you want to write down what I have to say?" he asked. I told him I would remember the information and write it down later. But it was clear that he was disappointed and rather hurt. As this incident indicates, by the end of my fieldwork people were accustomed to seeing me with a notebook; it had become my accepted role to write down what I observed and was told.

By the time I had spent five months in Benabarre there were no further problems in establishing rapport. From that point on I always had more offers of help than I could keep pace with. Any waste of time thereafter was due to my own shortcomings rather than reluctance on the part of villagers. I consider myself extremely fortunate to have studied a community where people were quite so willing to cooperate.

The reasons I was extended such generous help are various; an important one has to do with the tradition of Spanish hospitality. Courtesy and hospitality are hallmarks of Spanish culture, as foreign travelers usually find on their first day in Spain. Most Spaniards, whether in the cities or villages, take pleasure in being of service to foreigners who are visiting their country. We found this to be very much the case in our early stay in Benabarre. In the first few weeks, for example, I was not allowed to pay for my drink in the cafe. Any friend who was with me would insist on paying; even when I put up a struggle the bartender would allow my companion to win by simply not accepting my money. I was told, "When you're in our country we pay; when we go to your country we'll let you pay." This was somewhat disturbing because I could better afford the expense than most of them.

When I entered the homes there was the same concern to show hospitality. I could not simply enter and leave at will. I was given a seat and offered food and drink. To protest that I was not hungry or thirsty (and I often was not) was of no avail. The woman of the household would soon appear with wine, bread, and sausage meat, or depending on the time of day, with sweets and cognac. I learned to accept these offers gracefully, and always ate some part of the food, because it caused such visible distress when I refused. I was chided more than once that to refuse was to scorn (*despreciar*) their offer. There were times when I took some food or drink in four or more houses in an afternoon! Not surprisingly, stomach disorders were my most serious medical problem while in Benabarre. Nevertheless, it is not difficult to see how these patterns of customary politeness aided my work and provided a very genuine involvement with the people. To appreciate the importance of these customs one has only to contrast my experience with that of anthropologists in other countries, like Ecuador and Peru, where people have been known to run away, or lock themselves in their homes at the approach of the anthropologist!

*Use of Informants.* At this point I want to begin discussing some of the methods and techniques used in collecting the information. My fieldwork, like that of most anthropologists, consisted in two main techniques: use of native informants and participant observation. Here I will discuss my utilization of informants; later on I will have something to say about participant observation.

During the fourteen months I was in Benabarre I sought information from a large number of persons. I probably had random conversations with close to six hundred persons and held interview sessions with more than ninety individuals. Yet it would be misleading to suggest that these were of even approximately equal value to my study. The fact of the matter is that I spent as much as a quarter of my time with less than ten families. The latter were what I refer to as my "primary" informants—as distinguished from secondary ones.

Heavy concentration on a rather small number of informants was not a deliberate strategy when I began my work. In the first few months I attempted to extend my circle of intimate friendships as widely as possible, in the belief that I required a large sample of viewpoints to gain the knowledge I sought. I gradually relaxed this strategy, however, as I found that time spent in the company of certain persons was far more rewarding than in the company of others. The main criterion was simply how much I learned. I can remember spending a number of mornings with one of Benabarre's public officials, an extremely intelligent and congenial person. Yet at the end of the day, when I concentrated on writing up my field notes, I found that I had not learned a great deal. This particular individual was not deeply interested in Benabarre and could tell me relatively little about local affairs. He sought me out as someone with whom he could talk about international politics, life in America, or use as a sounding board for his opinions about who really assassinated president Kennedy. I had great difficulty guiding the conversation along lines more profitable to myself.

In this same period of fieldwork I met Antonio Marcial, a small farmer, and I began going with him daily to his fields. Antonio had a passionate interest in farming and in the whole range of problems facing the small producer—questions of vital importance to my study. I had all that I could do to keep pace with his insights and opinions. After only two hours with Antonio I might spend four hours elaborating my field notes. Quite naturally I began avoiding the official in favor of spending time with Antonio. More or less the same process of selection occurred with all of my primary informants. They were the persons from whom I gained the deepest insights and the most reliable information. Unfortunately the selection generated some hard feelings. A number of villagers became genuinely exasperated with me for preferring a certain person's company over their own. There were even times when jealousy over "possession" of me led to strained relations between erstwhile friends.

One other consideration influenced my choice of primary informants: this was

*Peasant-farmers eating their morning meal in the fields during the harvest season.*

a desire to represent certain occupations and levels of social position. The anthropologist is sensitive to the fact that persons in distinct social categories are likely to have different beliefs, attitudes, and opinions about the social order. Consequently I was as anxious to establish close ties to the high status landholding families as I was to Benabarre's peasant households. I eventually did secure a fairly good cross section of the community. By occupation my primary informants were: elderly retired peasant, young farmer, baker, shoestore owner, innkeeper, powerful landholding family, and college professor (see pp. 7-8).

My relationship to these persons was based on friendship. I did not follow the common anthropological practice of paying informants. Perhaps out of youthful idealism I had resolved before arriving in Spain that, if at all possible, I would avoid paying for cooperation. It was gratifying, therefore, to find that people were willing to go to considerable effort on my behalf simply because they considered me a friend. Friendship creates exceptionally strong bonds in Spain and as long as I could demonstrate the sincerity of my friendship I enjoyed the generous assistance of my hosts.

Working on this basis did, however, have certain drawbacks. One can obviously achieve greater efficiency if he pays informants for their time, releasing them from their normal economic concerns. In my case it was very different; I had to ask help in their free moments, or accompany them as they went about their daily affairs. Another problem was that there was always a certain degree of ambivalence in my relationship to informants because I was both *using* them and trying to meet the obligations of pure friendship. Even when we were relaxing in the cafe I would have questions to be answered, and my friends were aware that I was noting what was said and done. This left me open to the charge that I was simply exploiting the relationships for the information they could provide. I think at one time or another all of my informants must have doubted the sincerity of my friendship, and some expressed their doubts openly. José Pellicer said more than once that he suspected that if he were to stop aiding my work I would drop him like a hot potato. As time went on, however, I had opportunities to demonstrate my loyalty and regard for personal friends, so that there was a gradually diminishing concern over the sincerity of my motives.

I eventually developed a close intimacy with most of my primary informants. I could enter their homes whenever I wished, and I was at liberty to call on them for almost any kind of aid. There were even times when I felt I was treated as a genuine family member. One such memorable occasion was on a very cold night in January when one of my friends brought me the blanket from his own son's bed so that I should be warm. I had complained of being cold the previous night and I was thrilled to have an extra blanket. Unfortunately I had no idea where it had come from and I had to relinquish it that same night when his son discovered its absence. As my friend came back to retreive it I heard his wife shout after him, "You think more of that *americano* than you do of your own son!"

Most of my primary informants were remarkably protective of my interests. They made sure I was not taken advantage of, and that people dealt honestly with me. On one occasion I was sitting with two friends in the cafe. One of them was Señor Vicente, an elderly peasant who, for reliability and accuracy of detail, was a truly phenomenal informant. I was asking questions about something I had been told the day before about the period directly prior to the Civil War. It turned out that some of the information was wildly inaccurate. Señor Vicente became very annoyed and said angrily that whoever told me that did not know what he was talking about. The other friend, surprised at seeing Señor Vicente so upset, told him to calm down. With that, Señor Vicente slammed his huge fist on the table and shouted, "But I don't *like it* when they lie to him!"

Although I did not pay informants, I did give a good deal of attention to the matter of reciprocity. No fieldworker can expect to be always on the receiving end without giving something in return. I became aware that there were a number of small services that I could perform. Most of my friends did not have cars, so the offer to take them places was an obvious means of doing favors. I took them to Lérida or Huesca for visits to the social security clinics, for dental appointments, to attend to legal matters, or simply for shopping expeditions. When informants did not accompany me, they might ask that I perform an errand or purchase something for them in the city. Nor were these trips a waste of time from the point of view of my work. When I was accompanied by villagers they invariably took me along as they visited the homes of urban relatives and friends. It was extremely enlightening for me to be able to observe at first hand the social network ties that villagers maintain in the urban setting.

Other means of reciprocity consisted in giving occasional gifts: pastries, cigars, a bottle of cognac, toys for the children, or I might pay for a friend's drink in the cafe. I found, however, that villagers (except the very humble) would rarely allow

*Two of my villager friends. The man on the right was one of my primary informants.*

me to draw abreast of them in this reciprocity exchange. Villagers apparently expected very little of this sort of thing from me, so that even a small gift on my part sometimes caused consternation. I would realize that they thought I had done too much when they hastened to return the favor, such as insisting that I eat with them that afternoon or evening. So my attempts to redress the balance often resulted in deeper indebtedness.

It was evident that villagers (even those who gave very generously of their time) did not look upon me as someone to be exploited for material benefit. There were, however, certain nonmaterial rewards for them in our relationship. In the first place, I was a rather high status outsider by village standards. I was university educated and even though I insisted I was only a student, I was thought of, and invariably introduced, as a professor. The people of rural Spain have great respect for the "accomplishments of the mind" (see Pitt-Rivers 1954:71); consequently there was a certain degree of prestige to be gained simply from association with me, and from the fact that I valued their opinions and information. I also provided a certain entertainment function. To most villagers I was from a different world, and I could talk about unfamiliar subjects. I was constantly aware that people were anxious to engage me in conversation. This was even more the case in some of the remote hamlets where visits by outsiders, especially foreigners, are rare. When I would visit a household in these hamlets it was not uncommon for neighbors to drop in until the room was full of people eager to participate in the discussion.

The means I used for eliciting information ranged from structured interviews to casual conversation. Structured interviews (with a schedule of questions) were rarely employed within Benabarre, except for obtaining census data. But they were my main tool for interviewing government officials in Huesca and Madrid, and other high status individuals with whom I had only slight acquaintance.

Within Benabarre I sometimes used what I will call the "partially directed" interview. This was employed with close informants who had no objection to my writing in their presence. It was usually done with one person, but sometimes with two together. I used this technique when I wanted information on a specific topic, for example, on the yearly agricultural cycle, or in attempting to reconstruct a particular historical event. I would ask a series of questions and attempt to guide the conversation along lines which seemed most profitable. The important consideration in this type of interview was to have a series of topical questions thought out in advance. In the early stages of fieldwork I wasted hours of precious interview time by being insufficiently prepared. I would exhaust the few topics I hoped to cover and then would have to allow the conversation to wander. Afterwards, when I would rework my notes, I was chagrined to find that there were a series of questions I should have asked. I eventually found that an hour of prior preparation for this kind of interviewing was amply rewarded by the results.

Most of my information, however, came from far less structured situations. In the most typical interview I would meet an informant in his home (or sometimes in mine) and we would talk over a range of subjects. These were general topics and there was little advance preparation on my part except that I had a number of matters in mind which I wanted to discuss. I would be free to write and would take down my informant's comments as close to verbatim as possible—which was unfortunately not very close. These conversations often touched upon a series of delicate matters so it was best to keep the talks private, and to conduct them with one informant at a time. This was my most widely used and profitable interview situation.

I also gained a great deal of information from simple conversations in the bars, over dinner in the homes, or in the fields. In these situations I could rarely take systematic notes, but would jot down a series of comments in a pocket notebook. Sometimes these were totally spontaneous conversations, such as when I was but one member of a group discussing some recent event. On these occasions I was more of a listener than participant. At other times I would listen for hours, with only an occasional nod or exclamation on my part, as a villager poured out his troubles, or his hopes for the future. More commonly I would exercise some control over the conversation by asking questions and following up interesting comments. It is difficult to estimate the proportion of information which derived from these random conversations, but certainly a great deal. They were especially significant in providing new insights which could be followed up by more systematic interviewing at a later time.

There was one special type of group discussion which I found particularly rewarding. This type of discussion was with a circle of close friends with whom I met evenings in the cafe. The group of three or four men had been sitting together in the cafe for years, and I was only its most recent member. They were all exceptionally perceptive individuals who, due to their penchant for discussion, were somewhat derisively nicknamed "the philosophers." We would sometimes watch television, but the normal activity was conversation. I participated on about the same level as the others. I found it was quite simple to bring up subjects of interest to me to elicit comments and reactions. These were often matters of fact, such as what caused a particular village quarrel, which was the wealthiest family in Benabarre, and so forth. But on occasion I broached more crucial issues, such as mentioning a provisional interpretation of local social relations, or suggesting a low level hypothesis I was considering. My analysis of events sometimes brought vehement disagreement, and, less frequently, good enough arguments to dissuade me from that particular line of thinking. At other times my companions might agree and even add further confirmatory evidence. Regardless of the particular outcome, it was always enlightening to get reactions to some of my ideas and to see the degree to which my interpretations diverged from the way certain perceptive villagers viewed local social relations.

The *most* structured interviewing I carried out had to do with collecting census materials. There is nothing more crucial to effective fieldwork than accurate census data. It requires precise information and demands that one asks identical questions of every household. I wanted information on composition of households, ages of members, occupations, estimates of gross income, ownership of property, data on emigrant members, what jobs the emigrants performed in the cities, and so on. I plotted every household on a village map (drawn by myself) and then made out a separate notebook leaf for every household in the village. When I first began this project (in my second month in Benabarre) I thought I would have to contact every family individually. I was aware that this would take a great deal of time but reasoned that it would be an excellent means of establishing personal contact with a large number of people. This procedure resulted in almost complete failure.

I began one morning knocking at doors of selected households. I found mostly women in the homes (the men were in the fields) and they said I should return in the evening when their husbands would be there. When I returned I found the men equally hesitant to answer a schedule of questions, though they were always polite in excusing themselves. I gave up the whole approach after one dismal day, hoping that I could return to it later when there would be less suspicion surrounding my work.

I never returned to the project as originally conceived. As I gained skill in obtaining data from informants, I began to consider the possibility of utilizing them for census information. In a village of Benabarre's size people generally know a great deal about neighboring households. I reasoned that one informant in each of the four *barrios* (wards) of the village would be able to give me a great deal of information on the households of each area. I began with one of my best informants, an elderly peasant with a remarkable mind and memory. He assured me he could tell me everything I wanted to know about his *barrio*. I was amazed to discover that he not only could tell me about each household there, but about every farming household in the village. I later cross-checked some of the data with other informants and found that there were remarkably few factual errors in those data he surveyed. The rest of the census was done with five additional informants until I had covered the entire village. When completed it was incomparably more accurate and comprehensive than the official census done by the village government.

The success I achieved in tapping informants for census data led me to wonder why my anthropological colleagues often report that they visit individual households in gathering this kind of information. It would have been time consuming and very difficult to do so in Benabarre, and I would probably not have achieved any greater accuracy. Benabarrenses tend to understate their private resources and incomes when dealing with outsiders, whereas a person commenting on another household does not have the same inhibitions. The method I used not only saved time, but in certain respects may have enhanced accuracy.

Now that I have described how I utilized my informants, it will be useful to conclude the discussion with a few remarks on some of the limitations of the data they provided. The most important limitation is that informants can only present *their* view of the social order, which is usually not equivalent to that of a scientific observer. Benabarrenses, like all peoples, have sets of beliefs, opinions, and attitudes about their own culture which they express in word and deed. Unfortunately, these ideas are rarely at the level of analysis the anthropologist is seeking. This means that he cannot accept informants' statements at face value, and by no means as the finished products of his research.[2] Paradoxical as it may seem, *the native does not know his own culture*; at least he does not know it in an anthropological sense. The people of Benabarre are no better equipped to analyze their society than is the average American capable of writing a cultural analysis of American society. Some illustrations of this will make my meaning clear.

When I first investigated the matter of social differences and stratification I began by asking the admittedly naive question, "What social ranks or classes are recognized in Benabarre?" I expected from the answers to form some idea of the system of social ranking. No such system emerged. Almost all responses to the question were the same, that "There are no differences, we're all equals." This was the overwhelming sentiment, expressed by informant after informant. Yet I remained dissatisfied; it simply did not tally with my own observations. I had seen that certain persons were treated with a good deal of deference, their opinions were respected, their houses were in good order, and so forth. Then there were others who were not treated respectfully by anyone, their opinions were given little weight, their children went about poorly dressed, and they were quite poor.

I decided to put the difference between my observations and statements of villagers to a test. An anthropologist (Silverman 1966) who had studied stratification in an Italian community had carefully described a scheme for eliciting data on social rankings. It consisted of presenting cards to informants with the names of different individuals and having them say to whom they paid more deference or respect. I made up cards on all village households and asked the innkeeper, Ramón Pociello (who had earlier told me that all villagers were equals) to cooperate in the experiment. The first two cards I presented him were those of

---

[2] An important exception to this was the information provided by Don Tomás Mur (see pp. 7-8). Don Tomás was what may be termed an "analytical" informant. He was capable of standing apart from the social order and analyzing it in sophisticated sociological terms.

the village doctor and the village drunk, two persons whom I judged from personal observations were treated very differently. Ramón took one look at the names and in shocked tones said, "These two can't even be compared!" I asked, "Then they'll go in different categories?" "Certainly!" he replied. He then asked how many categories we would make. I told him that was entirely up to him. "Well in that case," he said, "I'll put the doctor (his card) on this end of the table and I'll put this drunk down here (on the other end); the rest of the community will all go somewhere in between." He eventually divided the households into six piles. When he had finished he apologized for having told me earlier that everybody was equal: "I've never thought of it in this way before; nor has anybody else in Benabarre!" I did the same card-ranking exercise with five informants and in every case it had the effect of making them aware that Benabarre was less homogeneous in terms of status than they had thought.[3]

A similar discrepancy appeared in my investigation of the inheritance system. I was consistently told that it was a rule that the firstborn son becomes the heir to all family property. Yet when I asked who had actually inherited in a series of sample households I found that as many as 40 percent of recent heirs had been females and youngest, rather than the eldest, sons. Again, people believed the system operated in one fashion and my analysis showed it to operate in quite another.

The foregoing examples contain the warning that the anthropologist must not confuse what informants *think* their culture is for what it is from the perspective of anthropological analysis. As one anthropologist (Bohannan 1963:10-11) has expressed it, there is in every culture a "folk" system of categories and beliefs which must always diverge somewhat from the "analytical" system constructed by the investigator. This implies that the conceptualization provided by informants is usually no more than a crude approximation of what the anthropologist is after. None of my village informants could have explained to me their system of social ranking; they are not sociologists and do not think in these terms. Nevertheless, by setting up the card ranking experiment I was able to elicit an underlying structure, which certainly existed, but of which most villagers were unaware. The anthropologist is continually searching for implicit patterns of this kind which may be only dimly perceived (if at all) by his informants.

*Participant Observation.* I now want to discuss the second main aspect of my fieldwork technique: my role as participant observer. To say that I was a participant observer means quite simply that I lived with the people and took part, to a certain extent, in community activities. This is an important part of anthropological field method because it provides the investigator with an inside view of the culture. Through participant observation he can know and experience the life of the people somewhat as the native does. This more than any other characteristic distinguishes the work of anthropologists from that of other social scientists; the anthropologist knows the people he writes about because he has lived with them and has shared their life.

I do not want to foster the impression that I merged with the community to the

---

[3] As this incident suggests, the anthropologist is occasionally responsible for altering the attitudes and outlook of the subjects of his study.

extent that I became one of them. It is important to state this clearly due to the widespread belief among persons with a tangential knowledge of anthropology that the anthropologist "goes native" in the field. In most cases such a degree of immersion in the community would make the investigator's work extremely difficult. A few examples will illustrate why this is so.

From the moment I entered Benabarre I was a rather mysterious and unaccountable phenomenon to most villagers. This was abundantly clear from the stares which followed me through the streets, the sudden silence of conversations as I passed, and from the wide-eyed amazement on the faces of village children. The sensation caused by my presence was convincing evidence, even at this early stage, that I would never be able to assume a status approximating that of a normal villager.

The initial shock of my presence eventually wore off, but by the time it did so I had taken on a special role in village life which also set me apart. I had become a university educated "professor" who was writing some kind of book on the village. There was no apparent means of avoiding such role-typing as long as I chose to be honest about my work. It may, for example, have been possible for me to have masqueraded as a tourist who simply wanted to spend a year in a Spanish village. But in order to persuade a community of suspicious people that I was a genuine tourist I would have had to *act* like one. This would have meant I could not ask detailed questions, take notes in public, carry out systematic interviewing, or go with peasants into the fields; such behavior does not conform to the expected tourist's role. To engage in such activities from that position would have aroused intolerable suspicion. It was far more convenient for me (as it must be for most anthropologists) to establish my role as *researcher* for what it was. Only in this way could my behavior be consistent with my explanation of it. Of course acknowledging my investigative role meant that I did not even appear to participate in activities in exactly the same manner as others. When I was not writing I was making mental notes or asking questions. The requirements of my role necessarily placed me at a certain intellectual distance from most activities.

Yet the benefits of having an openly acknowledged researcher role were obvious. Not only could I carry out my investigative aims openly, but I could depend on the cooperation of others. As my friends became aware of the kinds of things which interested me they would tell me in advance when a particular event would occur, or they would retain choice pieces of gossip, or try to recall for me a particular sequence of events. I obtained quantities of unsolicited information of this kind; this would not have been the case if I was not thought of as a scientific observer.

Another benefit of the researcher role was its flexibility. There were few norms and expectations in Benabarre as to what an anthropologist does, so I was able to define my role with considerable freedom. In Spain, for instance, persons of my social station (a college professor and wealthy by village standards) are expected to socialize mainly with persons of equivalent social rank, such as the town physician, lawyer, priest, or *secretario*. That I did not confine my friendships within such limits was initially perplexing, but was eventually accepted as part of my role. Thus when I was observed walking with a peasant and his mules, or listening to the village drunk in the cafe, villagers might smile but would characteristically shrug it off with, "Well, Ricardo's mission is to talk with everybody." With such a hazily defined position I could move between social strata almost at will. I never became identified with any social category to the extent that interaction with others was made difficult. Many times I spent the first part of an afternoon dining with the family of highest position in the region, and then spent the remainder of the day viewing pig sties built by some enterprising peasant. I was the only person (excepting priests) who had such freedom to move within local society.

Many anthropologists have expressed much the same idea on role flexibility by pointing out that the fieldworker's ideal is to be accepted as a "privileged stranger." He does not want to become so closely integrated into the social system that its rules, regulations, and taboos become binding upon him and restrict his activities. He is privileged in having a great deal of freedom to articulate with all segments of the society. And because he is only a sojourner, people are often willing to confide information to him which they would be hesitant to reveal to persons more firmly a part of the local scene.

I do not want, however, to overemphasize the social neutrality of my role in Benabarre. While it is true that I could deal with whomever I chose, the behavior of people towards me was invariably conditioned by their perception of my social position. In the eyes of villagers my university degree and profession demanded a certain measure of deferential behavior. In a Spanish village a person with university education commands considerable prestige; he is appropriately addressed with the honorific title *don*, and the respect for his educational accomplishments usually gives his opinions (on almost any subject) greater weight than those of others. The fact that I fell into this category had important implications for the way I was treated. Most of Benabarre's peasants did not remotely consider themselves my equal. When I entered their homes I was given the place of honor, the best wine, the newest plate, and the longest cigar. Peasants often felt it was inappropriate for them to be dressed in working garb as we talked, and often went to the trouble of changing clothes for my visit. Certain people could never bring themselves to use the familiar form of address (*tú*) with me—in some cases even after we had come to know each other quite well. Once when I asked a friend why he did not employ the familiar form of address he replied that, because we were not of the same social status (*categoría social*), it was not his place to do so. I asked him, "Then I have such high social status?" "Very high," he answered. My middle class American background made me rather uncomfortable in this situation, but I gradually learned to accept it as part of the local cultural definitions.

One incident is particularly engraved on my memory. It occurred when my wife and I were driving two villagers to Huesca, the provincial capital. We were on a mountain road and one of our passengers became carsick. Unfortunately we knew nothing about it because the poor fellow was unwilling to disturb us. I only became aware that something was wrong when the other passenger tried to open the back window of the car so that his companion could vomit. I looked back and saw the man desperately pressing a handkerchief over his mouth. I stopped immediately to let him out, whereupon he vomited profusely by the side of the road. I asked him why he had not told us he was ill. He answered that he had not wanted to inconvenience us, and humbly apologized for getting sick. We assured him that it was no bother and if he felt nauseous again to let us know immediately. He did get sick twice again, but said nothing; he simply endured it with the handkerchief pressed to his mouth. Fortunately I checked in the rear view mirror from time to time and when I saw him in this condition I would stop. Try as we would we could not get him to tell us. When I later told this story to my friends in Benabarre they explained that he was a humble and diffident person and it shamed him to cause us trouble. They conceded that he would not have been reluctant to admit he was sick if the driver of the car had been anyone from the local region.

The foregoing should give some idea of how I was regarded, and of the extent to which I was an actual participant in village life. The important thing to note is that the anthropologist does not have to merge with the community in order to benefit from participant observation. A great deal of the culture is effectively absorbed as one lives in the community. My only friends during those fourteen months in Benabarre were villagers; my only entertainments were their entertainments; I ate the same foods they ate; the only language I spoke was Spanish; even when I traveled outside of the village I was normally accompanied by villagers. With this degree of immersion a great deal of the culture was necessarily assimilated. Much of what I know about Benabarre today was never written down in my notebooks. Many details of everyday life became such commonplaces to me that I did not bother, or it did not occur to me, to record them. These things are familiar to me, not because I measured or quantified them, but because I experienced them.

Of course there is more to it than passive absorption. The anthropologist is also an active agent who must learn to maneuver effectively within the culture. He learns about certain cultural norms by having to manipulate them to achieve his ends. Some of my most reliable knowledge about the system of reciprocity and use of friendship networks derives from my experience in making contacts. I discovered that as long as I relied on relatively impersonal means of seeking cooperation I met with meager success. I carried a letter of introduction with me (from the University of Michigan) which I presented to a few officials in Huesca; and at various times I sought people out on my own, explained my purposes, and asked for their help. Relationships established on this basis were almost always a disappointment. When I was introduced personally, on the other hand, it was a different matter.

I once had the enlightening experience of utilizing both approaches with the same family. I had heard a great deal about a very dynamic *secretario* of one of the neighboring villages and I wanted to meet him, so I simply went to his home and presented myself. My reception was courteous but I found him to be rather suspicious and uncommunicative, so I did not detain him long. A few weeks later one of my friends in Benabarre suggested I should meet a relative of his who was a village *secretario*—the same individual. I replied that I had already met him and told of my experience. My friend insisted that things would be different if he introduced me. We drove over to the village that afternoon. The reception was a complete contrast to the earlier visit. There was no hint of suspicion; the wife served us coffee, cognac, and pastries while I had an informative conversation with the *secretario*. Afterwards he took me to the *ayuntamiento* and placed the community records at my disposal. He remained my best informant in that village.

From that time forward I abandoned the attempt to make contacts on my own. When I wanted to meet a particular individual I would find which of my close friends was on intimate terms with that person and would ask to be introduced. This was the only way I was able to meet some of the upper status families in the surrounding towns. It was also the most efficient means of dealing with officialdom in the provincial capital. I would arrange for Benabarre's *secretario*, or some other respected person to introduce me, and this never failed to open doors. As I used this strategy I was amazed at the extent to which network ties could be extended. By the end of my stay I felt that, with a little effort and cunning on my part, I could be introduced to almost any person in the region on a personal basis.

Finally, I want to make a few comments on the quality of my fieldwork experience. Hardly mentioned to this point is the fact that there was a great deal of personal trauma involved. Fieldwork may be both romantic and exciting, but it is also emotionally taxing. Throughout most of my stay in Benabarre I experienced a general anxiety about the progress of my work. I had received no formal training in anthropological field methods and I was never certain that my efforts were consistent with professional standards.[4] There was no doubt that I was collecting large quantities of data, and that I had established good rapport. But what was *not* certain was whether the materials would ever fit into a meaningful theoretical framework. Data alone, regardless of their quantity or intrinsic interest, are relatively worthless if they do not contribute towards some general interpretation. I had visions of returning to the United States with reams of data from which I would be able to extract nothing of great significance. I did, of course, have a general research design and concrete hypotheses to test, but the more I learned the more I was forced to adjust the goals of my research. And as new facts appeared various of my hypotheses began to strike me as either naive or meaningless. These continual misgivings made life in the village somewhat less than idyllic.

It may be that experienced fieldworkers suffer less from this kind of anxiety. Yet I am certain, after discussing the matter with many colleagues, that most novice anthropologists are highly anxiety prone in the field. As one writer (Pelto 1970: 224) has expressed it:

> Although solid data on this subject are scarce, widespread anecdotal evidence suggests that most fieldworkers experience periods of anxiety, depression, and helplessness, often accompanied by a strong tendency to withdraw from all data-gathering activity.

I also found it difficult to relax and to put the work temporarily out of mind. Even when I was not actively pursuing information I could not avoid making

---

[4] Until recently there has been widespread reluctance in many graduate departments of anthropology to provide instruction in field methods. The prevailing attitude seemed to be that fieldwork was not something that could be taught, and that each anthropologist would simply learn by experience. In the past decade this attitude has been widely challenged, and a growing number of anthropology departments have initiated seminars and experimental field sessions to prepare their students.

observations. Once made they had to be promptly recorded or the information would be lost. While I was in Benabarre no day passed (except when I was very ill) when I did not do some work on my field notes. The incessant work, and pangs of conscience when it was left undone, became a source of strain as the months wore on.

Late in 1967 I was forced to leave Spain for three weeks. The reason for the trip was to avoid paying customs duties on my automobile. The only way this could be accomplished was for me to remain outside the country for part of the month of December. I spent the period in the Pyrenees border state of Andorra. There I very determinedly concentrated on writing up some of my material in the form of a chapter to my doctoral dissertation. The writing proceeded remarkably well. Since I was totally removed from the community I was able to relax without a compulsive concern to write up observations. Moreover, the change of scene provided me with fresh ways of looking at my material. I wrote eighty-two pages in seventeen days, work which eventually became the nucleus of my dissertation. By the time I returned to Benabarre I had a far clearer notion of the direction I was heading and of specific research needs for the future. The Andorra experience gave me new confidence in my work; it also persuaded me that I would have to periodically leave the village if I hoped to analyze my material in any constructive way.

It was a similar consideration which led me to bring my fieldwork to a close after fourteen months. By that time data-gathering had clearly reached a point of diminishing returns. What I then required was time for reflection, library research, and writing. After a rather emotional farewell to my friends, I departed Benabarre on June 30, 1968.

# 2 / The background: prewar society[1]

The main concern of this study is with modernization, specifically the sociopolitical changes which have occurred in Benabarre in the last few decades. To fully comprehend the scope of change some historical perspective will be necessary. This chapter is therefore devoted to a description of the social organization of the "traditional" community—that is as it was before being significantly modified by the forces attendant upon industrialization. The account is based on the memories of elderly and middle-aged informants, and represents the time period from about 1910 to 1936.

## THE CLASS DIVISION IN THE PREWAR COMMUNITY

The people of Benabarre are aware that their community has experienced a fundamental social transformation in the lifetime of the present adult generation. They generally mark the change as having occurred with the Spanish Civil War (1936-1939). Before that conflict the community was dominated socially and politically by a small elite of professionals, officials, and large landholding families. This group comprised what is known in the sociological literature on Spain as the "rural bourgeoisie." Since the Civil War this class has dwindled in numbers and influence until today it is but a shadow of what it once was in Benabarre. The decline of the bourgeois elite constitutes the most significant social change to have occurred in the past century. It is the lack of such an elite today which makes the contemporary village so vastly different from what it was forty years ago.

The former importance of this class became evident to me very early in my stay. I found that almost any discussion of Benabarre's past led to reminiscencing about the politically influential personages of the prewar era, men remembered as *los señoritos*.

The striking fact about this memory, however, was the ambivalence expressed toward the former elite. Certain informants voiced admiration for the *señoritos* and deplored their absence today. Others remembered them less charitably, referring to them as *caciques* (political bosses) and exploiters of the poor, and insisted that

---

[1] The terms "prewar" and "postwar" in this account refer to the Spanish Civil War rather than to World War II.

the village was better off without them. An elderly storekeeper, representative of the former view, told me:

> You came forty years too late to write about Benabarre. There used to be real ladies and gentlemen here. They were important people who would really have known how to inform you; now there's nobody who's important at all.

Another informant remembered them less favorably:

> In the past the *señoritos* were in an untouchable position, the owners (*dueños*) of the village. They had their hands in everything. If I wanted to have a laborer work in my garden he would have to ask permission from the *señorito* first. . . . Before the war that's the way things were, the *señoritos* were literal *caciques*.

It was not, in fact, uncommon to have the same informant express these opposite viewpoints on different occasions. Once I was discussing the old days with the village blacksmith. He began relating numerous accounts of *cacicadas* (exploitation, unfair advantage) perpetrated by the lawyers; he did so angrily, his voice quavering with the apparent contempt he felt for them. I then asked if he felt they deserved the violence directed at them during the Civil War. His back stiffened and he said, "Certainly not! They were the finest people of the village. If Benabarre still had those *señores* today we would have a great village (*un gran pueblo*) here."

As I investigated the matter I found that the former elite had indeed been very influential, and that it consisted of men of much greater political stature than any in the contemporary community. The leader of Benabarre's Conservative party had twice been a minister in the national government; another was an ex-governor of the province of Valladolid; and there were others who played prominent roles in provincial politics. Even today the names of these important families recur frequently; some of the village streets are named after them, and certain of their descendants, though they no longer live in Benabarre, have become important figures in the larger society. There is also physical evidence of their former prominence. Certain houses of mansion proportions exist in the village which suggest the living style of a bygone era. They have vast numbers of rooms, are elegant in decor, have bells in various quarters of the house for summoning servants, and one even contains a private chapel. In the early part of this century these were the homes of the community's elite; today most of them are deserted, or inhabited only in summer when urban visitors descend on Benabarre.

In piecing together various informants' accounts of the period I gained a relatively consistent picture of the prewar community. It is clear that there was a two-class division to local society. On the one hand there was a small stratum of notables consisting, in the 1930s, of approximately twenty families, or about 6 percent of the village population. These were principally the town's professionals and civil servants: lawyers, physicians, notary, pharmacist, veterinary, property registrar, judge, *secretario*, postal administrator, and so forth. Also included, as marginal members of the class, were schoolteachers and certain wealthy merchants. This was the socially superordinate class which dominated Benabarre's public and political life.

The other class consisted of the rest of the community: shopkeepers, artisans, peasants, and laborers. Lumping all of the latter into the same class is not to imply that village society below the bourgeoisie was an undifferentiated mass. On the contrary, there were significant distinctions between, for example, the wealthiest shopkeepers and simple day laborers. Yet these were not distinctions of "class" in the same sense that this was true of the difference between the bourgeoisie and other villagers.

The term "class" is used here in a sense which includes consciousness of kind. The bourgeoisie thought of themselves as a group different from, and superior to, the rest of the population. Their unity and separateness from others was manifest in various recreational and social institutions. There was a *casino* which was a cafe–club for the exclusive use of the *señoritos*. The men would gather there to drink, read newspapers, play cards, and converse with friends. There was no firm rule that other villagers could not enter the casino, but as one informant observed, "They [the *señoritos*] wouldn't have kept a person out if he wanted to go; but nobody went there because we [ordinary villagers] would have felt out of place."

On festive occasions the bourgeois families held dances in the *casino* which were not open to the rest of the community. These dances were also attended by members of upper class families from the surrounding villages. The rest of the community held their festivities in the central plaza.

The most significant indicator of social distance was the rarity of intermarriage. Benabarre's notables sought marriage partners from within their class; marriages which crossed the class boundary were infrequent. Due to the restricted number of appropriate marriage partners within Benabarre the notables were obliged to seek spouses in other villages, towns, and even in the cities. The wife of one of

*A dynamic priest of one of the villages close to Benabarre. He has helped establish numerous agricultural cooperatives in surrounding villages.*

the lawyers was from the Pyrenean village of Benasque; the wife of the physician was from Madrid; the husband of the heiress of the village pharmacy was from the city of Lérida. All were, of course, of the same bourgeois social stratum. These examples illustrate the wide range and class-selected nature of the notables' marital ties. They were in sharp contrast to those of ordinary villagers who, in the vast majority of cases, took their spouses from within Benabarre or from villages in the immediate environs.

There was also a class-related difference in language. The notables spoke *castellano*, the official language of the country and the one common to all of Spain's educated classes. Even those bourgeois families which were permanent residents of Benabarre spoke Castilian. The ordinary villagers spoke *ribagorzano*, a language characteristic of all the villages in the immediate region. Almost all villagers could also speak *castellano* and this was the idiom used in dealings with the *señoritos* or with outsiders. *Ribagorzano* was considered, even by those who used it, as an unrefined peasant's dialect. Consequently it was below the dignity of the bourgeoisie.

The characteristics which most distinguished the elite from the rest were their education and professional careers. They were what are referred to in Spain as *gente de carrera* (career people). A career position can range from schoolteacher, or minor civil servant, to very prestigious professions like physician, attorney, or university professor. The distinguishing qualification is that the person have the necessary secondary or university education to fulfill the duty requirements of a bureaucratic or government post. In Spain during the 1920s only a small proportion of the rural population attained this level of education, and the majority were barely removed from illiteracy. Thus the difference between the educated and the uneducated was of profound social importance—as it is in most preindustrial societies where education is the property of a small privileged class.

Their education related the *señoritos* to the larger society in a fundamentally different way from that of ordinary folk. Benabarre's notables thought of themselves as part of a class (the provincial bourgeoisie) extraneous to Benabarre (see Pitt-Rivers 1954:77 for a similar class identification in Andalusia). This was the class whose members, in all large villages and towns, were the caretakers of national affairs on the local level. They identified closely with the values of urban–national society and lived as much in accordance with urban living standards as local conditions permitted. It is not too much to say that they thought of themselves as Spaniards first and as Benabarrenses second, whereas the identification of ordinary villagers was the reverse, as villagers first and as Spaniards second.

## THE GENTLEMAN COMPLEX[2]

One means of describing the bourgeoisie is to examine a key set of values which animated much of the behavior of members of the class. These values and attitudinal syndrome are what I will refer to as the "gentleman complex." In discussing

---

[2] This term is borrowed from Gilberto Freyre and Charles Wagley who have employed it to refer to a similar set of values among the Brazilian upper and middle classes.

this complex I will deal exclusively with the elite which epitomized these values. It should be understood, however, that the complex applied in varying degrees to all segments of prewar society; and, furthermore, remains influential in contemporary Spain.

The term "gentleman complex" refers to the fact that, in attitudes toward work and leisure, Benabarre's elite pursued a quasi-aristocratic ideal. They considered certain occupations and types of work to be below their dignity, and the performance of such labor entailed a loss of prestige. Of supreme importance in this evaluation was a disparagement of all forms of manual labor. It was thought demeaning for any member of the bourgeoisie to assume work which entailed strenuous physical effort, labor in the sun, or that involved dirt or soiled clothing. This also applied to domestic work; there were certain necessary household chores, such as fetching water, bringing in firewood, and feeding animals, which the notables could not dignifiably manage by themselves. Consequently all bourgeois households had maids and manservants to perform these tasks. Nor could they engage in farm labor, which, with its drudgery and association with animals, was the antithesis of dignified labor. The irony, however, was that many of the bourgeois families were among the community's largest landowners. The *ownership* of land, as distinguished from the working of it, held enormous prestige. The notables did not, therefore, actively farm their estates, except in the position of overseer. The actual cultivation was undertaken by tenants, day laborers, or through sharecropping arrangements with peasant households.

The negative attitude toward farming still prevails among segments of the upper class. One of the notable families (Casa Rivasés) still resides in a neighboring village but has declined considerably from its former position. The present family head does not have a profession and the family now derives their entire income from the land. When I was taking a census of the village I asked my informant if the head of Casa Rivasés actively engaged in farm labor. My informant, surprised at the question, answered in hushed tones, "Oh no! It would be degradation (*una bajeza*) for anyone of Casa Rivasés to till the soil!"

The most highly esteemed occupations were those which involved education and complex intellectual skills, such as attorney, notary, physician, and the like. These were "gentlemanly" occupations which allowed the man to wear coat and tie and set him apart from the surrounding laboring population. Education was the *sine qua non* for all professional and white-collar occupations, hence Benabarre's notables made strenuous efforts to educate their sons. Benabarre's school had only the primary grades, so secondary education entailed sending the children to schools in the towns and cities. It was at this time that the children of the elite began their apprenticeship in the norms and values of urban-national culture.

There was a decided effort to prepare the eldest (or the most promising) son to take over the father's profession, so that the first son of a lawyer was expected to become a lawyer and the son of a doctor a physician. Benabarre's elite was remarkably successful in maintaining occupational continuity. The town physician in the 1930s followed in the footsteps of his elder brother, father, and grandfather, all of whom had been the town's doctor before him. Another family had provided the village with three generations of lawyers. The pharmacist position was also maintained in succession from father to son. Thus the notables' commitment to education allowed them to monopolize the community's professional and career positions generation after generation.

Of course not all sons could inherit their father's position; many were obliged to emigrate and to establish themselves in the cities. There were also sons who, due to personal inadequacy or family financial straits, could not be provided with careers. There was generally an attempt to place such persons in the minor clerk and sinecure positions in Benabarre. If even this kind of work was unavailable the individual might not work at all rather than accept labor unbecoming to the family position. There is a famous story in Benabarre of a notable family which came on very hard times after the Civil War. The head of the household (a village official) was executed at the beginning of the war, leaving two spinster sisters with no support except a tiny income from a small amount of land. The two ladies had been brought up in an environment in which they had never worked, and even in these rather desperate circumstances they made no effort to improve their situation. In an attempt to help them, the manager of Benabarre's telephone switchboard offered them positions as operators. The ladies declined the offer as work inappropriate to their station. One of them died in Benabarre in extreme poverty and the other had to be removed to the poorhouse in Huesca where she died some years ago.

Another aspect of this gentlemanly set of values was a distaste for commercial occupations. Trade, with its avowed end of earning money, was stigmatized as crass and undignified. Business occupations were regarded, at best, as leftover possibilities

*A group such as this can be found playing cards in the central plaza on any warm afternoon from June until September.*

for those who could not attain the heights of a professional or government post. This prejudice prevailed despite the fact that commerce could be very remunerative. The two wealthiest families in prewar Benabarre were merchant households. Yet both had unsavory reputations for grasping and miserly behavior and neither was fully accepted among the bourgeoisie. In the eyes of Benabarre's elite, wealth alone was not sufficient to confer prestige and station.

The bourgeoisie was also Benabarre's principal leisure class. Their employment of servants freed them from the many common tasks incumbent upon others. Also, most worked only sparingly at their professions because there was a limited amount of administrative or legal work to be done in a small community. Thus a characteristic of the class most commonly remarked by my informants was their conspicuous consumption of leisure. Here is how a reliable informant described the daily schedule of one of Benabarre's important lawyer-politicians:

> He was sort of a lawyer but he didn't work at the profession a great deal. . . . It was a compliment in those days to say a man didn't have to work very much. . . . His day went something like this: after getting up at about 11:00 a.m. he would go to the pharmacy of Don Martín who was the most important political figure in the village then. They would have a *tertulia* (conversation with a circle of friends) and at about 1:00 p.m. they went for coffee in the *casino*. Afterwards they went to meet the mail bus to get the daily newspaper. They would talk awhile there and then might go to the plaza. . . . He wore a coat and tie but always went sloppily dressed with stains on his clothing. He never had much money and lived modestly.

For the most part the notables were admired for their ability to avoid a constant round of work. There was little suggestion of the notion, common in countries where a "Protestant ethic" predominates, that hard work lent a man dignity and self-respect. The notables, like all villagers, worked for the concrete goal of maintaining an appropriate standard of living for their families. To exert oneself beyond such a goal would have occurred to them as unnecessary and a bit foolish. Relaxation from work, rather than causing pangs of conscience, was considered the just reward of status and social position.

A final element in what I am calling the gentleman complex was the elite's special concern for refinement and learning—summed up in the Spanish term *cultura*. Ideally, a "cultured" person was one who had delicate manners, good breeding, and who cultivated a knowledge of literature and the arts. Bourgeois homes contained modest libraries with books on literature, religion, and history. The leisure they enjoyed was considered a necessity if the person was to properly "civilize" himself. On the contrary, labor, especially physical labor, was thought to brutalize. As one of the modern representatives of this class exclaimed in reference to Benabarre's farmers, "How can they be anything but brutes (*brutos*) if all they do is work the land?"

In practice probably very few of Benabarre's notables possessed *cultura* in the sense of erudition and scholarship. But they had been exposed to Spain's educational system which championed literary and humanistic learning, and they were more knowledgeable of Spanish high culture than the semi-literate villagers around them. Their superiority to others in this regard is reflected in the term *gente de cultura* (cultured people) still used by villagers in reference to the former elite.

## INTERCLASS RELATIONS

I have described, up to this point, a rather clear-cut differentiation in the prewar community. Yet one should not draw the conclusion that this status difference was associated with a high degree of interclass segregation. There were, it is true, certain social and recreational activities (see pp. 25-26) in which the bourgeoisie was set apart. But these examples of social exclusiveness were far less important in the total structure of prewar society than the enduring, and often intimate, relationships which prevailed between the upper class and large segments of the lower classes. These relationships were what are known as patron-client ties.

A number of authors (particularly Pitt-Rivers 1954, and Kenny 1960, 1961) have pointed up the significance of patron–client relations in binding the upper to the lower classes in Spanish society. In prewar Benabarre these relations were a principal nexus of the social order and merit examination. One of the main characteristics of patron–client ties is that they are based on the acceptance of *in*equality; a powerful and socially superior individual assumes the role of protector and benefactor to persons who are his social inferiors. He becomes a father figure and treats them as if they were somewhat less than fully mature adults. The relationship is ideally accompanied by a sense of *noblesse oblige* on the part of the patron, meaning that he recognizes an obligation to exhibit generosity toward the humble and poor. The client must reciprocate, for the contract entails obligations on *both* sides; he usually works for the patron or serves his interests in various other ways.

Another characteristic of patron–client ties is that they are highly personalized. They are what anthropologists refer to as "multiplex" relationships (Bailey 1971: 304-05). Each individual generally becomes closely involved in the private life of the other. Thus an employer–patron is not only related to his employee on a labor contract, but becomes engaged in other spheres of his life, such as acting as personal adviser, lending support in family crises, and the like. In Benabarre the personalized nature of the relationship is suggested by the terminology employed. The only phrase I ever heard my elderly informants use to characterize their relationship to the former *señoritos* was that they had close friendship (*mucha amistad*) with them. And the term a client used in reference to his patron was *padrino* (godfather).

The latter term suggests the paternalism involved. Consider, for instance, the situation of a maid in a notable household. Her function was to handle the household drudgery. Yet this economic tie was invariably converted into a complex social relationship. In return for dutiful service the family assumed obligations toward her which would otherwise have been the responsibility of her natal family. They stood guardian over her personal morality, saw that she attended church regularly, supervised her courting, and would often play an important role in arranging her marriage. Her personal ties to her employer were often extended to include other members of her family. The *señorito* might, for example, help her brother find employment or intervene on the side of her father in a neighborhood quarrel.

Perhaps the best way of characterizing these relationships is to present biographical data from certain informants who helped me construct a picture of the prewar society. Their relationships to the *señoritos* were fairly representative of those of a majority of villagers in that period. The accounts illustrate the intimate contact with the notables and the continual resort to their influence in crisis situations.

The first account is that of Ramón Brualla, a peasant now sixty-three years old. His family owns a modest patrimony, about 25 hectares, which they formerly supplemented by sharecropping part of the estate of one of Benabarre's lawyers. The sharecropping arrangement in Benabarre was a contract whereby a landowner apportioned the land, half of the seed, and half of the fertilizer; a peasant household provided an equal share of the seed and fertilizer and all of the labor necessary to cultivate the land. The produce was then divided equally between the two parties. In formal terms it was a commercial relationship; in practice it became far more, with the sharecroppers tending to become social appendages of the landowner's household. Ramón remembers with some pride that he was free to come and go in the lawyer's house as he pleased, and says that he was on friendly terms with all members of the family. After finishing his work in the fields he and his father would go to their employer's house to clean pig corrals, feed his animals, or do any odd jobs he might ask of them.

Ramón and his father were also part of their landlord's political clientele. In the prewar period there was considerable political factionalism in Benabarre and each of the major politicians maintained large blocks of supporters among the peasants and workers. These supporters were expected to vote as the patron wished and to take his side in political disputes. Ramón's lawyer–patron was one of Benabarre's most active *políticos*. On various evenings during the week he would meet in his home with his workers and trusted followers to discuss village political events. Ramón and his father were expected to take part in these meetings (called *tertulias*). They served as listening posts and informers (*alcahuetes*) for the lawyer of moves by the other faction, or of anything said or done in the community which might be of political significance. When the lawyer became mayor, Ramón's father was named councilman in the village government. It was apparently of no concern that he was barely literate; he was placed there (as were others) because he could be depended upon to rubber-stamp his patron's actions and decisions.

In return for these various services Ramón's family was rewarded by the lawyer's protection and patronage. Ramón recalls that his father once injured a neighbor in a freak accident; the head of the axe he was using flew off its handle and struck the man with whom he was working on the forehead. The latter took Ramón's father to court to sue for damages. Ramón's father was represented by his *padrino* in the case and as Ramón remembers, "That guy [their lawyer–patron] was so clever that even though my father was guilty we won the case and got off scot-free." Ramón himself was once caught by the Civil Guard on a poaching charge. Their *padrino* again intervened and was able to have the fine reduced to a nominal sum. Then when Ramón was drafted into the military service his *padrino* visited him in the camp at Zaragoza. Ramón recalls that he complained to his *padrino* that he did not like his duty assignment or his outfit. The lawyer said he would see what could be done. A few days later Ramón was transferred to a new company where, as he says, he had almost nothing to do for the remainder of his term in the service.

A relationship of this kind continued as long as both parties felt that the services received were equal to, or outweighed, those rendered to the other. If, however, one of the parties failed to meet these expectations, the relationship was jeopardized. This occurred between Ramón's father and his *padrino* during the political unrest of the Republican period (especially the years 1934-1936). The leftist political agitation had the effect of heightening sensitivity among Benabarre's peasants to possible exploitation of them by the *señoritos*. This enhanced awareness is reflected in Ramón's disgruntled comment on their unrecompensed obligations as sharecroppers:

> In those times we used to go to his [the lawyer's] house at night to clean up his animals and feed them. This was after a hard day's work, and we never got paid a cent for all of that.

As a consequence of this growing resentment Ramón's father became less willing to do his patron's political bidding. The issue came to a head in the elections of 1936. As Ramón recalls:

> Don Antonio [the lawyer] came to our house asking for our vote, telling us that he would either have our vote or he'd kick us off the land [meaning he would give the sharecropping rights to some other family]. My father said he'd be willing to make a deal: he'd give his vote to Don Antonio and his wife's vote to the father of Tobeña [the present mayor]. But Don Antonio wasn't satisfied with that. He wanted both votes or nothing, and went away mad. And sure enough, he took away our sharecropping rights.

The second account to be detailed is that of Martín Zanuy who was one of the village barbers, and a bartender prior to the Civil War. Martín became closely associated with Benabarre's property registrar, a powerful village official. The relationship began quite simply: Martín was struggling to make a living as a barber and was helped considerably by the generosity of this official. Martín commented:

> Don Custodio was a real friend of mine. When he came in for a shave he paid me five *pesetas* when the price was only one-fourth of a *peseta*. That was twenty times the actual cost! He was what I call a genuine *señor*. He was very generous and was always good to the poorest people of the village.

Around 1930 when Martín became a bartender, Don Custodio secured for him the position of concierge in the *casino*. Martín was responsible for the upkeep of the *casino*, served drinks, and was in daily contact with all of the most important men of the village.

The generosity with which Don Custodio treated him placed Martín deeply in his debt. Thus when his *padrino* became embroiled in the political turmoil preceding the Civil War, Martín was obliged to lend assistance. Don Custodio led a group which carried out acts of defiance of the leftist dominated village government and Martín was an accomplice, even though he had no taste for politics. As he explained to me:

> I was not a *político* then nor will I ever be one. I didn't want to get mixed up in those things [politics during the Republic] but I had to get involved. I didn't have any choice. I simply did what those who gave me bread told me to do. What else should I have done? . . . . Don Custodio and the others in the *casino* gave me my living and I had to do for them whatever I could in return.

The biography of José Pellicer, now seventy-seven years old, illustrates the very considerable dependency on the elite common among poor villagers. José was the second son of a nearly landless peasant household from which he received no property inheritance. In early adolescence he attached himself as a manservant (*criado*) to a wealthy household. He grew to manhood there and was apparently treated well, somewhat like an inferior member of the family. He says today that he came to regard himself as more a part of that family than of his natal household. When he was in his early twenties he turned to the wife of his employer (rather than to his parents) for assistance in arranging his marriage.

After marriage he established an independent household but continued working as a day laborer for two of the notables. By parsimonious living he was able to accumulate sufficient wealth to begin a career as a moneylender, at first modestly but eventually on a large scale. When he encountered serious difficulties in collecting debts he asked the assistance of his *padrino* who would often exert moral pressure on the delinquents to expedite repayment.

José claims that he had only one serious encounter with the law in his lifetime. The day after he was inducted into the army he became involved in a heated argument with a corporal which ended when José struck him in the face. The corporal pressed charges and José was in very serious trouble. He sent word of his predicament to his *padrino* in Benabarre who, through his influence with high ranking military officials, succeeded in having the charges dismissed. As José related this account he ended by comparing the contemporary village unfavorably with the past:

> In those days there were men here who were really worth something. If you got into any kind of trouble they could get you out. Today there's nobody who can help you.

These biographical fragments should give some picture of the close association and interdependence between the classes. They should also make clear that the promise of political support was one of the crucial links in the chain of reciprocity. Electoral politics were of preeminent concern to the bourgeoisie, so much so that they are often remembered as *la clase política* (the political class). Until the Republic in 1931, the notable families were all affiliated with one of the two national political parties, the *Conservadores* or *Liberales*. These parties were opposed in national and local elections and their village representatives were pitted against one another for electoral support. Benabarre's notables were divided approximately evenly between the two parties, a circumstance which caused endemic village factionalism. Each of the major party leaders (principally the lawyers) had large numbers of supporters, both in the community and in surrounding villages. In an election he secured the promise of their votes and was able to pledge them in support of his party's candidates. The prize was control over local government. The victorious faction was able to staff the government and various official posts with friends, relatives, and supporters. Politics was a serious matter because the power of office was unabashedly used to serve the interests of the in-group and to punish the opposition.

Ordinary villagers were only indirectly involved in this political system. Their vote was to meet a personal obligation to a patron rather than to support a party, issue, or platform. As an elderly villager told me, rather impatiently, when I asked him to which party he belonged in the old days:

> I didn't belong to any party, nor did any of the lower class (*la parte baja*)....
> We didn't know anything about politics; we don't understand those things; that was for the *señoritos* to worry about. We voted the way they asked us to.

The patron–client attachments that have been described are crucial for understanding prewar society. Benabarre was organized to a very large extent in pyramidical fashion. The strategic ties in the social system were those which bound members of the lower classes to their *padrinos*. These ties, in the normal order of events, took precedence over those which bound them to neighbors and friends. There were various ways in which this vertical structure of society was manifest. There is the evidence, first of all, from interpersonal relations. One of the outstanding characteristics of the period, remembered vividly by every informant, was the almost interminable legal wrangling among the peasants. Benabarre's court was the scene of constant juridical struggles as villagers did battle with each other over disputed boundaries, an errant animal, threatening remarks, unintentional injury, and the like. When there was any kind of quarrel between two villagers, rather than attempting to settle the matter among themselves, there was a tendency for each to run to his lawyer–patron for advice and support. The lawyers would generally exaggerate the issue, and the case would go to court. There is a nearly unanimous opinion in Benabarre today that the lawyers took unfair advantage of their clients in these disputes. They encouraged the ire of neighbor against neighbor for their own political and pecuniary ends. "In court the two lawyers would pretend to hate each other," said one informant, "and then they'd get together in the *casino* and laugh over how they plucked the feathers of some ignorant peasants."

Indicative also of the hierarchical nature of the community was the absence of any organization or grouping of ordinary villagers independent of the bourgeoisie. There were no labor organizations or lower class political groupings, and the one attempt at a cooperative was organized and staffed by members of the bourgeoisie. Benabarre's peasants and workers were organizationally amorphous except when they coalesced by virtue of individual ties to a common patron. Thus on all controversial issues the community tended to divide along factional lines with one notable and his followers allied against another notable backed by his supporters.

There is one important caveat to add to this discussion of interclass relations. Patron–client ties were not equally characteristic of all segments of the community. The peasants, laborers, and very poor were far more likely to have enduring relations with a *padrino* than were the well-to-do merchants or livestock dealers. There were a number of reasons for this. In the first place, for patron–clientage to operate there must be a wide disparity of social status; the client must be willing to play the role of child to his social father. There was not sufficient status differential between Benabarre's wealthy merchants and the bourgeoisie to make such a relationship appropriate. Many of the merchants were the economic equals of the bourgeoisie and were independent of them occupationally; they did not cultivate their land and their sons and daughters did not become servants in their homes. And finally, their commercial operations led them to considerable involvement with the world outside the village. They had to form contacts with city merchants and they came into association with a wide range of persons in the course of their business activities. And because, as we shall see shortly, an important function of the bourgeoisie was to monitor relations with the supra-village society, the merchants were less in need of this service than other segments of the community.

## THE NOTABLES AS "BROKERS"

Notwithstanding that there were varying degrees of dependency on the bourgeoisie, all villagers—including merchants—had recourse to their influence at one time or another. The notables could perform certain services for people which the average villager had almost no means of accomplishing. Their ability to do these favors, and the considerable power they commanded, had to do with their special relationship to the larger society beyond Benabarre.

Benabarre's bourgeoisie were what anthropologists refer to as political and cultural "brokers." The term refers to those persons, particularly in peasant cultures, who serve the interests of communication between local communities and the urban–national society (Wolf 1956; Silverman 1965). Broker relations tend to be found where a nationally oriented elite resides in close proximity to a community oriented peasantry. Members of such an elite thus participate in two worlds: they identify closely with the culture and institutions of national society, and they know how these institutions operate; at the same time they are part of the personal world of the village. They are therefore in a favorable position to perform two functions, both of which redound to their power: they are the principal means through which villagers attempt to deal with the society beyond the village; and they are able to influence the way in which national institutions articulate with the local community.

The latter aspect of their role was obvious: the *señoritos* were terminal points on the governmental and ecclesiastic hierarchies which extended down to Benabarre from the cities. The parish priest represented the power and authority of the church; the judge occupied the final position on the juridical ladder from Madrid; Benabarre's lawyers were local representatives of nationwide political parties. Thus whenever a villager had dealings with administration or officialdom—to register his land, to use the courts, or notarize a document—all such acts filtered through the hands of the notables. The capability of controlling these institutions was an enormous source of power. Those in control of village government could lessen or increase a man's tax burden. Obtaining justice in the courts depended as much on the state of one's personal relationships to lawyers, judge, or even court secretary, as on the merits of one's case.

There was another aspect to this broker role which had less to do with formal institutions. As previously mentioned, the notables maintained far more extensive network ties outside of Benabarre than ordinary villagers. They gained these networks through their wider participation in the larger society, by marital connections, from schooling, and through occupational contacts. Consequently, even in situations in which they had no formal authority they could often reach centers of decision making by personal contacts. Accounts of how two of my elderly informants avoided military service illustrate how this system of informal influence operated.

Joaquin Marcial became eligible for the military draft in 1920. Conscription was based on a lottery system and Joaquin had drawn number four, virtually assuring that he would be among the seven or eight boys called up from Benabarre. Yet Joaquin's family, a needy peasant household, was reluctant to part with his services for the two years he would spend in the military. They sent Joaquin to discuss the matter with Don Vicente, the village physician. The doctor admitted that he had no power to affect the matter. He did, however, have an old friend from medical school who was then director of medical operations for Huesca province; this man had the authority to declare men physically unfit for military service. Don Vicente and Joaquin traveled together to the provincial capital where the doctor renewed friendship with his former classmate. As a favor to his old friend the medical director certified that Joaquin had defective vision (apparently a false certification) and he was relieved of his military obligation.

Another of my elderly friends escaped military service (again extralegally) when one of the village lawyers wrote him a letter to be delivered to the lawyer's cousin, an army general in Barcelona. After reading the letter the general procured my informant a certificate of physical ineligibility, and he was free to return to Benabarre. My friend recalls this event with wonderment: "That's what those men could do; a few strokes of the pen and I was out of the military!"

Also by virtue of supra-village contacts the notables could aid villagers in tapping employment opportunities in the larger society. Girls of peasant families were often placed as maids in the homes of the notables' urban relatives. One of Benabarre's lawyers was known to have excellent connections with officials in the Civil Guard, and he was able to place boys from Benabarre in that organization.

It was the ability to influence people and institutions in the larger society which made the *señoritos* an important resource for others. Even those who were not dependent upon them economically found it expedient to remain in their good graces. Villagers were continually disposed to perform some small service for the *señorito*—giving him gifts of food, performing some chore, sending a child on an errand for him—in order to maintain a viable reciprocity relationship. One man recalled his childhood in the early 1930s:

> I remember my mother was always sending me with gifts of food for the big people (*los pudientes*); and in those days we hardly had enough to eat ourselves. But that's the way it was, all the poor folk thought it best to stay on the good side of those people in case they got into trouble, or had a favor to ask.

## THE SECOND REPUBLIC AND CIVIL WAR

The society I have described existed until the latter stages of the Republican period (1931-1936). At that time certain significant changes began to occur in the community, changes which were in large part a reflection of political events occurring throughout the larger society. The Second Republic was an interlude of genuine parliamentary democracy in Spanish politics. It was a time when groups representing all segments of the political spectrum were given unprecedented freedom to advocate their programs and philosophies. The unforseen, and unfortunate, result was a steady polarization of the country into two irreconcilable political camps on the left and right. Benabarre experienced a similar evolution: in 1931 the notables were the effective caretakers of a rather quiescent village politics; by 1936 new groups had arisen, adamantly opposed to the *señoritos*, and had gained control of village government.

When villagers are asked why the political atmosphere changed so rapidly in this period they usually attribute it to campaign oratory and to the new leftist organizations established in the community. One informant said it was a matter of "opening the eyes" of the people:

> Things changed because the eyes of the peasants were opened. There were lots of meetings by people from outside of the village, telling us that things should be changed, that they couldn't go on like this. All these speakers came to open the eyes of the people. . . . I heard some of them . . . some things I liked and some I didn't. When they spoke against religion I didn't like it. But when they attacked *caciquismo* [boss rule by the *señoritos*] I heard it and I liked the one who spoke up against the *caciques*; he was from Barbastro. But with all this happening the hatreds increased here.

Villagers had always held specific grievances against the elite, against venal lawyers, sham elections, and political bosses. The tendency, however, had been to accept these evils as an integral part of all politics. It was startling and illuminating, therefore, when leftist spokesmen began to articulate these resentments as part of a general political program. Most villagers found themselves nodding in agreement when an orator said that *caciques* had exploited them, or that previous elections had been fraudulent.

The fact that aspects of the leftist program were appealing should not suggest, however, that a majority of villagers declared their support. Most of the people of Benabarre remained skeptical of all political promises and preferred to have as little to do with politics as possible. The new groups on the left thus constituted a small minority of the total population, just as had the support for the politics of the elite.

The national political parties which achieved some success in Benabarre were the Socialists (*Unión General de Trabajadores*) and the *Falange*, the Spanish fascist party. A number of villagers associated with the Socialists established a *Centro Republicano* (Republican Center) which was intended as a "worker's" *casino* in opposition to that of the notables. It was a meeting place for all persons of leftist political persuasion and contained socialist literature to be read by anyone interested. In turn, many of the *señoritos* of the original *casino* swore fealty (apparently in secret) to the *Falange*, the most dynamic new group on the right.

In 1935 and early 1936 the political atmosphere became increasingly embittered. The notables led a boycott of a foodstore owned by the family of a schoolteacher who had become Benabarre's most influential spokesman for the political left. Then after the leftist–Republican forces gained control of the *ayuntamiento* in 1936, the *señoritos* and their followers defied the government by secretly placing *Viva Cristo Rey* (Long Live Christ King) signs on the walls of the town hall. The rancorous atmosphere of the village was recalled by a notary from Madrid who had happened to arrive for a summer vacation in Benabarre just a few days before the outbreak of the Civil War:

As soon as I arrived I saw that the town had completely changed, that it had undergone a great transformation. There were people who refused to greet me, people I had known and been friendly with for years. These were part of the lower class who now saw in me another *señorito*. Previously I had always dealt with everybody, I was not at all political nor were any of my family. Now it was different . . . there was a complete division of the village; and because I was a notary I was put in a new category and treated differently.

General Franco's military uprising against the Republic began on July 18, 1936. Since early in that year Benabarre's town hall had been controlled by the leftist faction which had come to power through the "Popular Front" (*Frente Popular*) victory in the national elections of February, 1936. The election had enabled them to temporarily replace the *señoritos* as the managers of village government. Due to this control by the left, Benabarre was to remain loyal to the Republic during the Civil War. When news arrived of Franco's rising, the village government sent the Civil Guard to arrest persons thought to harbor anti-Republican sentiments. These were virtually all of Benabarre's *señoritos*. Only males were arrested, however; their families were unmolested. About a week later armed members of the FAI (Federation of Iberian Anarchists) arrived in Benabarre. These were members of liquidation squads from Catalonia who had gone from town to town executing "enemies of the revolution," which in practice meant the bourgeoisie. With help from a handful of Benabarre's leftists they removed the fifteen detainees from Benabarre's jail, drove them to a point two kilometers below the village, and executed them. Some days later another lawyer was shot and a few others were executed when the war took a bad turn for Republican forces in Aragon. The list of persons executed included two priests, three lawyers, the registrar, pharmacist, veterinary, *secretario*, physician, and three minor civil servants. Others killed were either closely connected to the Church or they were victims of personal vendettas against them by some of the principal leftists.

The people of Benabarre were deeply shocked by the executions. For days afterward the village took on the appearance of a ghost town as people locked themselves in their homes, afraid to venture into the streets. There had perhaps been a considerable number who applauded when the notables were jailed; but almost none had foreseen such a drastic outcome. "The first days of the Civil War were like an exciting game," said one man, "but when the executions took place we suddenly realized it was for real!"

The class-directed violence of the Civil War was to have a profound impact on village social structure. The main representatives of the class which had controlled local society for at least the past century were suddenly removed. For the first time in modern history Benabarre had no clearly defined sociopolitical elite. In succeeding years new members of the bourgeoisie would take up residence in Benabarre. But representatives of that class would never again command the political importance of the prewar *señoritos*. Certain technological and economic changes began to occur in the postwar which totally undermined the basis of the earlier political system. It is to this economic and technological revolution that we now shift our attention.

# 3 / Benabarre in the rural revolution

Before dealing with the important demographic and technological changes occurring in contemporary Benabarre it will be instructive to say something about the source of these changes, the industrialization of Spanish society.

## INDUSTRIAL DEVELOPMENT IN SPAIN

There is a widespread popular image of Spain, among Americans and Europeans alike, as a country which in recent times has experienced little fundamental social change. This image derives, I believe, from the conservative, even traditionalist, nature of the Spanish government. Since the Civil War the country has been under the authoritarian rule of Generalísimo Francisco Franco. This government has declared itself a monarchy; it has made every effort to extirpate the liberal–leftist influence of the Republican period; political parties have been abolished; there are no open elections; and genuine labor unions and strikes are prohibited. A major governmental priority has been to reassert the authority of the Roman Catholic Church throughout Spanish life, and particularly in the educational realm. Above all, the regime has made an iron commitment to the maintenance of public order and is intolerant toward any kind of group demonstration or public expression of dissent. These major policies make the regime appear anything but progressive; certainly alongside the liberal democracies of most of Western Europe, Franco's Spain is a political anachronism.

Yet the image is deceptive. Despite its ultraconservative political stance, the Spanish government has made vigorous efforts to create a modern economy. The program of industrialization, which includes development plans similar to those of socialist countries, has been carried forth with remarkable success. Spain has achieved in the last two decades levels of national growth greater than in any other period of its modern history. In the ten years from 1957 to 1967 the economy grew at the unprecedented average rate of nine percent annually, one of the highest rates of development in the western world (Anderson 1970:xiii). Per capita income surpassed the six hundred dollar level in the 1965-1966 period, removing Spain from classification as an "underdeveloped" country (Anderson 1970:218-19).

These events have had a dramatic impact on the life of the average Spaniard. Twenty-five years ago Spain was a fundamentally rural society in which approximately half of the population was engaged in agricultural occupations. By 1971 a majority of Spaniards lived in urban areas and more than two-thirds of the labor force worked in industrial or service occupations. In 1950 the country was only incipiently mechanized; no automobiles were manufactured within Spain and there were only 90,000 passenger cars in the entire country. In 1970 alone Spain manufactured 450,400 automobiles. In the same year there was a car, truck, or motorcycle for every seven persons in the population (*Anuario* 1971:164). Thus in twenty years the country has been transformed from a nation of pedestrians into one which suffers from urban traffic congestion, parking problems, and inadequate highways. Mechanization has arrived in the countryside with similar abruptness. Most of Spain's farmland was cultivated by animal power in 1950. As late as 1959 there were only 33,000 tractors in Spain as a whole. A decade later it was estimated that by 1971 the number of tractors would reach 300,000 (*Informe Sociológico* 1970:226).

It would be inaccurate, however, to convey the impression that the country's industrialization is wholly a product of recent decades. The beginnings of Spanish industrial growth date back to the middle of the nineteenth century. There were periods of vigorous expansion at the end of that century and in the early decades of the present one. Particularly notable were the periods of growth during World War I and the industrial boom in the 1920s under the dictatorship of Primo de Rivera. But despite this general progress, the pace of Spain's development lagged considerably behind that of the advanced countries of northern Europe. Throughout the nineteenth and the first third of the present century Spain had one of the lowest standards of living in Europe, high rates of illiteracy, and, comparatively speaking, feeble industrial production. The famous writers and statesmen of the "Generation of '98" constantly bewailed the *atraso* (backwardness) of Spain and proposed remedies for national regeneration.

Unfortunately, in the first half of the twentieth century such regeneration (at least in terms of material progress) was not in the offing. In 1929 Spain reached a plateau of industrial growth which was not to be surpassed again for another quarter century (Roman 1971:19). The world depression impaired the economy in the early 1930s and before there was time for significant recovery the nation had embarked on the disastrous course of civil war. Spain emerged from the conflict in 1939 with large parts of the country devastated by war and economically exhausted. Recovery was further impeded by the involvement of the rest of Europe in World War II, making economic normalization impossible. Moreover, after the World War, due to the Franco government's earlier association with the Axis powers, Spain was ostracized from the community of nations. She was cut off from normal sources of international commerce and did not receive Marshall Plan aid; as a result her economy was virtually stagnant throughout the 1940s. Spain's international standing changed for the better in 1953 when, due to Cold War concern, the United States signed bilateral aid agreements with Spain in exchange for military bases. Also in the early 1950s Spain began to benefit from the tourist trade which was eventually to become a principal source of the revenue employed to finance industrial expansion.

The unparalleled economic takeoff of the contemporary period can thus be partially explained by the fact that Spain is catching up on developments which, without the Civil War and its aftermath, would have occurred earlier and at a more gradual pace. At any rate, it is certain that Spain is now, for the first time since the beginnings of the industrial revolution, gaining ground on the more advanced countries of Western Europe. In the remainder of this chapter attention will be focused on the far-reaching impact that the country's rapid industrial growth has had on the Spanish countryside.

## THE RURAL EXODUS

The most fateful consequence of industrial expansion for Spanish villages has been the associated rural to urban emigration. The trend in itself is not new; since the latter part of the nineteenth century there had been a gradually accelerating transfer of population from the Spanish countryside to the cities. In the late 1950s and 1960s, however, the movement swelled to massive proportions. It is estimated that in 1963 alone there was a net transfer of 154,000 persons from towns of less than 10,000 population to urban areas; in 1964 the figure was 180,000 (Anlló-Vázquez 1966:97); in 1970, 141,000 (*Anuario* 1971:54). Between 1960 and 1970 well over a million villagers deserted their homes for life in the cities.

The effects of this massive emigration on country districts has often been catastrophic. The movement is known in Spain as the "rural exodus" (*éxodo rural*) and it is appropriately named. Reports from Navarra and the Basque region tell of entire communities being abandoned and then sold by the former inhabitants. The same has occurred in Castile; and even the traditionally large communities of Andalusia and Estremadura now often hold only half of the population they contained a few years earlier.

Severe depopulation is also occurring in Huesca province in which Benabarre is located. The province is basically rural, with more than half of the population residing in communities of less than 2,000 inhabitants. It is therefore reasonably representative of the many largely rural provinces in Spain which are losing population to the industrialized regions of the country. Between 1955 and 1970 Huesca province suffered a net decline of approximately 10,000 persons. Global provincial statistics, however, because they also include the expanding urban areas, do not indicate the magnitude of flow from the countryside. To gauge the extent of this emigration one must look to some of the hinterland areas of the region.

In the summer of 1971 I visited a number of small peasant hamlets to the north of Benabarre. The hamlets are located in a relatively isolated area. None are situated on the main highway which traverses the region and they are only connected to the highway by very rough dirt roads. The nearest town of any consequence is Benabarre, which is about ten kilometers distance from the nearest of these hamlets and about thirty kilometers from the farthest. In each community I compared the 1950 census figures with the population totals in 1970. Most of the figures derived from *ayuntamiento* records; where these were unavailable I carried out a household census with the aid of informants. The table on the following page summarizes the findings for seventeen villages.

The comparison shows a tremendous depopulation in a relatively short period. The area as a whole has lost 61 percent of its population in twenty years! Some communities (Mongay, Almunia, Chiró, Mora) are now completely abandoned

42   BENABARRE IN THE RURAL REVOLUTION

*The exodus from the countryside is depopulating entire villages. This photo shows the ruins of deserted homes in a village 20 kilometers from Benabarre.*

and a good many others (Chiriveta, Estall, San Lorenzo, Colls, Torre de Baró) are very likely to become extinct in the near future. Some villages have been deserted so recently that only the boarded-up windows and the total silence belie the impression that they are still occupied. In the now deserted village of Almunia I met

DEPOPULATION OF VILLAGES, 1950-1970

| Village | 1950 | 1970 | % of pop. loss |
|---|---|---|---|
| Caladrones | 178 | 122 | 31 |
| Ciscar | 87 | 65 | 25 |
| Antensa | 42 | 29 | 31 |
| Sagarras Bajas | 80 | 59 | 26 |
| Luzás | 181 | 58 | 68 |
| Alumnia | 39 | 0 | 100 |
| San Lorenzo | 37 | 8 | 78 |
| Chiró | 40 | 0 | 100 |
| Torre de Baró | 40 | 13 | 70 |
| Mora | 17 | 0 | 100 |
| Colls | 41 | 18 | 53 |
| Viacamp | 95 | 47 | 50 |
| Literá | 93 | 28 | 70 |
| Mongay | 25 | 0 | 100 |
| Chiriveta | 51 | 7 | 86 |
| Estall | 69 | 3 | 92 |
| Montañana | 160 | 34 | 79 |
| Total | 1275 | 491 | 61% |

a man who used to live in one of the nearby hamlets. He now lives permanently in the city of Lérida but has become the caretaker of village lands, commuting about once a week to do the necessary work. He told me that as late as 1960 Almunia was an apparently flourishing community. "Then around 1962 or 1963," he said, "everybody got emigration fever; six years later there was hardly anybody left."

The villages which retain parts of their population offer nearly as disheartening a spectacle as the deserted ones. Here and there one finds an occupied house; it is usually surrounded by others which are deserted and boarded shut. Many of the latter are in advanced stages of deterioration; the walls are crumbling and many of the roofs have caved in. Still others have been converted into corrals for pigs and chickens. It is not at all uncommon to find livestock now kept in rooms where a family lived only a few years ago. Young people are conspicuously absent in all of these villages; they have either found employment in the larger towns or cities or they are studying in secondary schools. Thus elderly and middle-aged persons make up a large proportion of the residents. In many of the villages I surveyed, 45 percent of the population was over fifty years of age; in one village I found an astounding 60 percent of all residents to be over fifty! Not surprisingly, the occupants who remain are extremely pessimistic about the future. In my conversations with villagers I encountered only a few individuals (all of them elderly) who expressed any determination to stay. All others thought their villages were doomed and said they too expected to emigrate sometime in the future.

The above description is of a very small area of the province. Yet more or less the same conditions prevail in all of the genuinely rural districts. In my travels throughout the Pyrenees region I invariably found that the more isolated and smaller the community, the greater was the depopulation. The tendency everywhere is for people to move from smaller to more urban centers.

The larger villages, and those located on major transportation arteries, are not as seriously affected. Many of these villages are, like Benabarre, losing population; but rarely are they declining to such an extent that their existence is threatened. The rate of desertion is not as great as from the smaller communities and the larger centers are often recipients of some of the migrants from the surrounding hinterland.

Benabarre's population statistics are indicative of the trend occurring in many of the villages of its size throughout the province. The following table records the town's population for every decade since the beginning of the century.

BENABARRE'S POPULATION, 1900-1970

| Year | Inhabitants |
|------|-------------|
| 1900 | 1,819 |
| 1910 | 1,880 |
| 1920 | 1,730 |
| 1930 | 1,664 |
| 1940 | 1,544 |
| 1950 | 1,356 |
| 1960 | 1,260 |
| 1970 | 1,022 |

The 1,880 inhabitants recorded for 1910 probably represent the greatest population in the town's history, the culmination of a gradual growth during preceding centuries. After that time there is a steady decline. In the sixty years from 1910 to 1970 the village lost approximately 45 percent of its population. The loss is readily visible in the town's physical aspect. All of the back streets have numerous houses which are closed. Out of a total of 374 dwellings in the community, approximately 100 are uninhabited.[1] This means that slightly greater than one out of every four houses in Benabarre is unoccupied.

While the empty houses make it evident that many whole families have departed, most emigration from Benabarre has not been of this kind. It has rather been of parts of families; the young people have been the most disposed to leave while their parents remain in Benabarre. The occurrence of this single member emigration has been so widespread that virtually all of Benabarre's adults have either children, or siblings, or other immediate relatives, who live in the cities or large towns. The walls of the dining rooms of most village homes are dotted with photographs of children, or brothers and sisters, who live elsewhere—in Barcelona, Manresa, Sabadell, Zaragoza, or some other city.

A breakdown of the community's population in terms of age reflects the desertion by the young. In 1965 only 36.2 percent of the population was under thirty years of age. This is considerably below the figure for Spain as a whole which lists a full 50 percent under thirty. Benabarre's decline in this respect has been sudden; as recently as 1950, 45 percent of the village residents were under thirty. At the other end of the population curve, as might be expected, there is a high percentage of elderly persons. In 1965, 32.4 percent of the inhabitants were over fifty. This is appreciably higher than the figure of 22.5 percent over the age of fifty for Spain as a whole (*Anuario* 1968:50).

## THE CRISIS OF THE SMALL PROPRIETOR

In determining the causes behind this large-scale desertion of the region it is important to distinguish between two different classes of factors which encourage emigration. There is, first of all, the rather obvious fact that people are being drawn out of the village by the wide range of employment offered in the cities. Benabarre's young people are particularly attracted since they are the ones most capable of taking advantage of the available opportunities. Moreover, if they have received an education they must necessarily emigrate if they hope to secure a white-collar position appropriate to their level of schooling. But quite apart from the economics of emigration, most young people leave the village by choice. The average adolescent far prefers the stimulating atmosphere of the cities to what he considers a monotonous and restricted life in the village.

On the other hand there have been many persons in the last few years who have left Benabarre reluctantly. Their basic motivation for leaving has been that they

---

[1] These houses are not, however, crumbling into ruins as I have described for the isolated hamlets. Quite the contrary, they are rapidly being renovated. See below, pp. 57-58.

can no longer make an acceptable livelihood in the community. There are large numbers of peasant proprietors, craftsmen and agricultural laborers who have increasingly found themselves in straitened circumstances. Household enterprises which have passed from father to son for generations have suddenly been undermined by forces emanating from the larger society. I will discuss these forces shortly. The point to be emphasized here is that emigration from Benabarre and the surrounding region has been encouraged from *two* sides. Villagers are not only being drawn out of the community by opportunities in industry; they are also being pushed out by a very substantial breakdown in the traditional economy.

This economic breakdown applies most directly to small peasant proprietors, but also to craftsmen such as copperworkers, sandalmakers, weavers, and the like. Many of these households have left the area entirely and of those which remain a majority have gone into serious decline. It is when one examines the situation of these families that he forms an impression of the true revolution which is occurring in Benabarre. These households formerly made up the middle range of local society; they were owners of property and of an ancestral house which usually dated far back into the village past. The peasant households have been the backbone of agricultural production for centuries. Suddenly, within the time span of one generation, a majority of these households have either disappeared or it has become apparent that they are no longer viable enterprises.

A survey of the community's peasant households reveals their adverse circumstances. In 1968 there were 117 households in Benabarre which could be classified as farming families, in the sense that more than half of their household income derived from agriculture. Of this number, 53 (or 45 percent) were "incomplete" in such a way that they will be unlikely to continue in the next generation. Eighteen of these households have male heirs who have not married and will have no issue. There are thirty-five others consisting solely of elderly or middle-aged couples who have no heirs to carry on the household tradition; their children have either emigrated, are being educated, or have taken up some nonfarming occupation.

But even the large number of incomplete households does not indicate the full extent of the problem. Virtually all of Benabarre's peasant farmers face difficulties in finding heirs to continue the family tradition. The example of Casa Moreta[2] illustrates the problems faced by many. Casa Moreta is a five-member household composed of a middle-aged couple, their nineteen year old son, a girl of seventeen, and another boy of eleven. They own 22 hectares of good land, a team of mules and they have some livestock. This was a patrimony which, only a few years ago was considered substantial, far better than the average holding. The household head, Manolo Sopena, wants his eldest son to inherit the property and continue working it as he has. His son, however, has different ideas; in direct opposition to his father he has refused the inheritance and has taken on a job as an apprentice stonemason. The boy says he would be willing to become a farmer if he could own a tractor, but he absolutely refuses to cultivate the land with mules. For him, as for most of Benabarre's youths, to work the land with mules is degrading. His

---

[2] Nearly all households in Benabarre are known by a nickname which differs from the family name. Hence this household is known as Moreta, while the family surname is Sopena.

*Members of a farm family eating their nightly meal.*

father cannot buy a tractor because the family property is insufficient to make it a worthwhile investment. The daughter is being courted by a shopkeeper's son and she will leave the household at marriage. Manolo hopes that his youngest son will remain in the household, but it is unlikely that they will be any more successful in holding him than they have been with the eldest. Manolo is grieved by the possibility that he may not have an heir to follow him. He remarked to me ruefully, "I can't understand young people today. I had to practically fight my brothers for the inheritance; now I can't even get my son to take it!"

Another household, Casa Juanico, is one of the moribund ones mentioned above. It consists of four persons: a middle-aged man and wife, their bachelor son (now thirty-one years old), and the man's elderly mother. Like Casa Moreta, a little over a decade ago this was thought of as a house of substantial means. I once listened to two elderly peasants as they discussed the old days in Benabarre. One of them remarked that when he was a young man houses like Juanico, with about 20 hectares, seemed like great landowners. "Nowadays," he said, "what we thought was a good patrimony is so small that nobody wants it." At the present time the young man of the household works the family lands only occasionally. He has become a tractor driver for the farming cooperative and earns a decent salary. His father does most of the work tending the family farm and livestock. The tragedy of Casa Juanico is that the son remains unmarried. The family has sought desperately to find him a wife, but with no success. He courted a girl some years ago but she ultimately rejected him in favor of the village electrician. She did so after heeding her family's warning that life as an electrician's wife offered a better prospect than becoming a drudge in a peasant household.

The fact that the young man of Casa Juanico has been unable to find a wife deserves additional comment. His is by no means an isolated example. Besides Juanico there are seventeen other peasant households in Benabarre which are headed by young men who cannot find wives. In the last fifteen years all peasants of the region have experienced a severe "bride famine"[3] as local girls have become increasingly unwilling to marry into peasant households. Benabarre's farmers are acutely aware of the difficulties they face. One peasant told me:

> About ten years ago the girls around here [Benabarre and environs] started refusing to marry into peasant houses. So we had to arrange matches between our boys and peasant girls from villages up in the mountains. But now you can't even find them. They'd rather serve as maids in Barcelona than marry our boys.

Actually, the eighteen bachelor heirs in Benabarre is a small number in relation to the extreme difficulty peasants (even the largest property owners) are experiencing in finding women. In the last few years villagers have even been driven to the extreme of advertising their situation in agricultural journals and in Church-sponsored magazines. They place a notice in the journal which states that they are seeking wives, and they briefly describe their personal and economic circumstances. By these means a few families have contacted women from other (usually poorer) regions of Spain who feel they can improve their situation by marrying into Benabarre. At least three marriages have taken place as a result of this kind of advertising. However, the most important reason that there are not more bachelor heirs is that many young men, realizing that they had little chance of attracting wives as farmers, have emigrated to the cities.

It is apparent from the preceding discussion that peasant agriculture is singularly unattractive to Benabarre's young people. It is important to emphasize, however, that this is an entirely new situation. Only fifteen years ago it would have been virtually unheard of for a potential heir to refuse the family inheritance. It would have been an equally rare circumstance for a healthy heir to property to be unsuccessful in attracting a wife. Nowadays these are common occurrences.

There are a number of reasons for this drastic shift in attitudes toward farming. Throughout the remainder of this section I will analyze some of the forces which have combined to undermine the position of the traditional farm family in Benabarre. As will be seen, most have to do with the small scale of household production. The impact of agricultural mechanization illustrates some of the difficulties.

The first tractor came to Benabarre in 1955. Since that time thirty-four more have been purchased by villagers. By 1970 approximately 90 percent of the village lands were worked by machinery. Even the many households which do not own tractors have taken to hiring them from neighbors or from the agricultural cooperative. Except for a few conservative old men, everybody in Benabarre now agrees that mechanized agriculture is the only way to farm successfully.

Despite this admission, a majority of Benabarre's farmers cannot own the machines which have become the necessary means of production. The small size of most farms make tractors a prohibitive investment. Some notion of the small scale of household agriculture in Benabarre can be derived from statistics in the follow-

---

[3] This is the term used by Edward Norbeck for the same phenomenon in rural Japan. See *Changing Japan* (New York: Holt, Rinehart and Winston, 1966), pp. 55-56.

ing table (calculated from the *Primer Censo Agrario de España, Año 1962*, pp. 52, 53, 66, 67).

SIZE OF LANDHOLDINGS IN BENABARRE

|  | No. of owners | % of owners | % of land |
|---|---|---|---|
| Less than 10 hect. | 145 | 56.5 | 6.6 |
| Between 10-50 hect. | 82 | 32.0 | 26.5 |
| More than 50 hect. | 29 | 11.5 | 66.7 |

As the figures indicate, more than half (56.5 percent) of Benabarre's landowners own fewer than 10 hectares. However, these figures include all of the community's landowners rather than just the 117 households which I have classified as farmers. If only the holdings of farm families are calculated a figure of between 15 and 17 hectares is derived as the median household farm.

This is far short of the amount of land necessary to carry on mechanized farming.[4] The agrarian extension agent for the Benabarre region estimated that at least 50 hectares are needed to make use of a tractor feasible. A tractor is an expensive piece of equipment which inevitably represents a loss to its owner if it remains idle through most of the year—as it must if it is used only to work, for example, a 20 hectare farm.

From my own observations in Benabarre it appears that the extension agent's figures may be somewhat high, and that farmers with more than 40 hectares are able to profitably employ machinery, at least for the present. Of the thirty-five tractors in Benabarre only a handful are owned by households with fewer than 40 hectares. Most of the latter make a profit from their machines by using them to haul materials for the building trades as well as working other people's land through sharecropping and rent agreements.

Using the minimal figure of 40 hectares, there are only about thirty households in Benabarre which have sufficient land to support mechanization. The large majority of peasants, at least 70 percent, cannot hope to mechanize their individual farms. Consequently, in the last few years all but the largest landowners have found themselves without the means of production to carry on farming as independent units. The small farmers ordinarily rent the necessary machinery; but of course this involves a profit for the tractor owner, making production costs for the small farmer greater than they would be if he owned his own equipment. All of Benabarre's farmers recognize the advantage that mechanization has provided the large owners. One of the comments I heard most often while in Benabarre was the expectation that a few large landowners would eventually triumph at the expense of the others.

Mechanization has also vastly reduced the need for labor on small holdings. Before the advent of machinery a 20 hectare farm required the labor of two men,

---

[4] The situation is made more complex by the fact that all agricultural holdings in Benabarre are fragmented. Virtually none of the farmers have all of their land in one place; they own a strip here, another on the other side of the village, and so forth. Such a pattern of landholding reduces the efficiency of machinery.

usually a man and his son. Today the owner of a farm of the same size, who hires tractors and harvesters, does not require the services of a second laborer. One man, even an elderly one, can tend to the livestock and to the residual farm chores which cannot be handled by machines. His son is more profitably employed in some other trade, as a stonemason, carpenter, road construction employee, or similar occupation. By 1971 almost all of Benabarre's small holders had bowed to this economic logic, and father-son teams had virtually ceased to exist among the small and medium farmers. Benabarre's household agriculture is now overwhelmingly in the hands of middle-aged and elderly men while their sons work at some other trade, are being educated, or have left the village entirely. The chance that some of these boys will eventually return to the household is remote. After a few years working at a trade the boy usually discovers that he earns more than his father, and also that he derives greater prestige from his new occupation. His withdrawal from agriculture then becomes permanent.

Although mechanization is a very serious problem, it is only one among a whole series of difficulties occasioned by the small scale of peasant farming. Another has to do with the discrepancy between the limited resources of farm households and the vastly increased demands being placed on them at the present time. The same households which are too small to support mechanization have likewise been unable to keep pace with the general rise in standard of living which has taken place in the last few years. In order to understand the impact of this rise in living standards it will be necessary to briefly examine the kind of living which has traditionally been associated with Benabarre's household agriculture.

The most striking characteristic of the traditional peasant economy was that it was based on ascetic living and strictly limited consumption. When peasants describe what life was like in the past they invariably preface their remarks with a commentary on the extremely parsimonious living. "We hardly saw money in those days," is a common observation; or "The peasants of this village buy more items in two weeks now than they used to buy all year."

Granting that this may entail some exaggeration, it is nevertheless true that peasants got along with very few money expenses. A household with a 15 to 20 hectare farm could meet most of the food needs of a five member family on its own resources. Each family maintained an irrigated kitchen garden which produced virtually all the vegetables (beans, potatoes, cabbage, tomatoes, lettuce, etc.) and fruits eaten during the year. The average farmer also owned wheatfields, vineyards, and olive groves. The wheat, when traded to the baker in the form of flour, was their source of bread. The vineyards produced grapes, wine, vinegar, and raisins; the olives produced their oil. The annual slaughter of the household pig was the main source of meat yielding salted hams, pork rind, and various types of preserved sausages (*chorizo, longaniza, salchicha*). Fresh meat and eggs came from the rabbits and chickens kept by every household, and on important festive occasions a lamb might be slaughtered. With a rather unvarying diet, still adhered to by many peasant families, the inventory of food items to be purchased was limited: salt, sugar, dry salted fish (*bacalao*), and a few additional foods were the only outside needs.

Cash income derived from the surplus production of cereals, wine, oil, or sale of livestock. Money was required to pay for specialist services from physicians, stonemasons, blacksmiths, carpenters, and so forth. There was also the need to provide dowries for non-heir children and to pay taxes. Expenditures on entertainment were limited to major annual festivals or perhaps an occasional visit to the cafe. Family members wore one or two sets of clothing throughout the year, with another set for holidays. Children occasioned few expenses; quite the contrary, they were looked upon as economic assets and were expected to contribute to the prosperity of the household as early as possible. Education beyond the elementary grades was out of the question. As soon as a boy had mastered the rudiments of reading and writing he was put to work in the fields. Girls were sent at adolescence to serve as maids in the homes of the wealthy. Store purchases were generally avoided. According to an oft repeated refrain, *"Quien a la tienda va y viene, dos familias sostiene"* (One who goes frequently to the store supports the storeowner's family as well as his own).

It was by all accounts a very frugal existence, as it *had* to be if five or six persons were to live on very slight resources. Minimal consumption was, in fact, a *sine qua non* for the continuation of this system of agriculture. The main peasant virtues extolled thrift, hard work, early rising, and the like. The lazy person, or one who was saddled with *vicios* (literally "vices," but meaning simple personal indulgences like tobacco, drink, spending on luxuries, and so on) was thought certain to bring his house to ruin.

This pattern of living is still possible on the same size farm today. The land will provide all the food, shelter, and elementary requirements which it did thirty

*A middle aged couple rest on their balcony and converse with passersby.*

years ago. There are, in fact, various elderly couples in Benabarre, and more in the surrounding villages, who continue to live in almost precisely the manner I have described. They cultivate a few plots of land, keep chickens, rabbits, a household pig, and have a vegetable garden. By leading an extremely parsimonious existence, with no luxuries or entertainments, and minimal expenses, they manage to scratch out a living. In the home of one old couple with whom I am familiar the only amenities are running water and electricity. They have no toilet, no furniture, they cook over a wood fire on the hearth, their house has not had repair work done for a generation, and the two of them go about in ragged and patched clothing. The man once boasted to me of his ability to live economically, saying he has not entered Benabarre's cafes for twenty-two years. This is the only existence he has known and the fact that other villagers have begun to live differently does not disturb him.

Benabarre's young people, however, find such an existence totally unacceptable. In the last two decades they have been exposed to a series of cultural influences which have drastically altered their view of what constitutes a proper living. What the parents considered a reasonable standard of living now appears to their offspring as abject poverty.

This, then, is the crux of the matter: traditional household agriculture is not disintegrating because the average peasant can no longer make a living. There is nobody starving in Benabarre or even suffering serious privation. In fact villagers almost unanimously say they live better now than at any time within memory. The problem is that while small-scale farming will provide for subsistence and a simple living (as it always has), it is far less capable of providing for the new consumer goods, diversions, and educational demands which have become minimal expectations in the last fifteen years. It is this fatal discrepancy between the new demands and the traditional means of satisfying them which has brought the demise of so many long-established households.

## METROPOLITAN CULTURE AND THE URBAN IMPULSE

The foregoing discussion highlights the fact that increased demands and quest for a higher standard of living have contributed significantly to the disintegration of the peasant economy. These new demands have arisen, in the main, from the impact on Benabarre of what I will refer to as "metropolitan culture."

The term simply denotes the mainstream culture of the larger society and it is used here in contrast to the folk or peasant tradition of the village. Throughout Benabarre's history there has always been an important difference between village culture and the norms and standards associated with urban society. Patterns of dress, manners, speech, and various local customs diverged significantly from those encountered in the cities. Indeed, the contrast between *señoritos* and peasants described in the preceding chapter was primarily a difference between the norms of the larger society and those of the village. It will be recalled (pp. 26-29) that Benabarre's prewar elite was described as an essentially urban-oriented class and as embodying the values of national society. The rest of the village, on the other hand, lived much less in terms of metropolitan standards and were basically community oriented. Today this distinction has been virtually erased; "village culture" has retreated on all fronts while the tastes and living styles of the old bourgeoisie have become common aspirations of a majority of the community.

The change is due to the fact that Benabarre is no longer set apart from the main currents of national culture. Industrial technology and the communications revolution have vastly reduced the physical and psychological distance between the village and metropolitan areas. Radios and television, expanded travel by bus and automobile, the wide diffusion of mass consumer goods, frequent contacts with urban friends and relatives—all have operated to reduce or eliminate the barriers of rural isolation. Benabarre has, in effect, been incorporated within the orbit of the nation's urban-industrial centers.

This new proximity between Benabarre and metropolitan areas has had an enormous impact on the way villagers evaluate their personal circumstances. The community and life there has been placed in a direct frame of comparison with the cities and larger towns, so that villagers are now led to contrast their situation to that of people very much like themselves who live in urban centers. Such comparison has presented them with a wide range of alternatives to the encysted life of the past, and there can be no doubt that this has raised the level of dissatisfaction with village life as a whole.

There are various reasons for this discontent, one of the most important being that in Spain (and the same is true of most developing countries) there is a considerable lag in the spread of modern conveniences in the countryside relative to the cities. Facilities such as telephones, central heating, modern bathrooms, secondary schools, and commercial entertainments are far more accessible in the metropolitan areas than in rural communities. When, for example, a village family emigrates to Barcelona they almost inevitably move into an apartment which is furnished with a higher level of physical amenities than the home they occupied in Benabarre. In the cities there are also schools close at hand so that urban families have a reasonable opportunity of providing secondary education for their children. In Benabarre, and in most Spanish towns of its size, there is no school beyond the elementary grades. Secondary education for village children therefore entails the additional expense of supporting the students away from home in the provincial towns or cities.

Certainly one of the complaints I heard most frequently from villagers was that their urban relatives live better than they do. A man who was made the sole heir to the family property in Benabarre made this comparison with his brother who now lives in Barcelona:

> My brother left Benabarre twenty years ago practically a pauper. Now he earns more money than I do, he owns a car, and his family has lots of things we don't have.

And another:

> People who used to live here in wretched poverty (*con miseria*) now come back from the cities bragging about how much better they live than we do.

As the second comment suggests, the invidious comparison between city and village is reinforced in encounters with urbanites. During my stay in Benabarre I witnessed dozens of meetings between villagers and their urban relatives. On a majority of these occasions the city people adopted patronizing attitudes toward various aspects of village life (ranging from complaints about "unhygienic" conditions to criticisms of the pettiness of village social relations) and spoke glowingly of benefits they enjoy which are unavailable in the village. Villagers rarely, if ever, put forth counter arguments in defense of the community.

The difference between city and village is not, however, only a matter of amenities. Urban living (as villagers perceive it) also entails a very different mode of existence. The work engaged in by city people is thought of as less arduous and as "cleaner" than work performed in the village. The cities also offer a greater range of entertainments and means of spending leisure time. Compared with the variety of activities in the cities, village life appears uneventful. As one teenager expressed it, "My cousin in Barcelona goes to a dance or football game every week. Here in Benabarre there's nothing for us to do." Closely related is the deep appreciation almost all villagers feel for a particular quality of city life, usually referred to as *animación* (life, activity) or *ambiente* (lively atmosphere). The terms refer to the fact that city streets and cafes are full of people, there is a constant bustle of activity, and there is the ongoing spectacle provided by the coming together of different kinds of people. The quiescent routine of country life is the antithesis of these desired qualities.

Life style considerations such as these have been especially influential among Benabarre's young women and are part of the explanation for the "bride famine" mentioned earlier. Village girls have become extremely sensitive to the different possibilities which await them if they marry within or outside the village. It is no exaggeration to state that, other things being equal, most girls in Benabarre would rather marry an urbanite than a villager. The girls are often quite candid about this preference; the twenty-year-old daughter of a peasant explained to me why she was not responsive to the attentions of a suitor from one of Benabarre's wealthy farm families. She said that marriage to him would involve her in a type of life which she wants to avoid:

> I've lived this life [in a peasant household] and I don't like it. One of my sisters is married to a factory worker in Monzón [a large provincial town] and lives in an apartment there. She doesn't have to feed pigs or go around in sloppy work clothes all the time like we do around here. She dresses up every day and spends afternoons walking the children and promenading (*de paseo*) with her friends. That's the kind of life I want too.

These comments were made in 1968. When I returned to Benabarre for a short visit in the summer of 1971 this girl was living and working in the city of Andorra, and had met a boy there whom she intended to marry.

Cases like this are becoming legion in Benabarre. In 1967 a marriage was planned between a girl from a small peasant village to the north of Benabarre and the heir to a farm household in Aler (the satellite hamlet attached to Benabarre administratively). The couple had been engaged for a number of years but the marriage had been delayed due to the girl's hesitancy to become the wife of a farmer. She attempted to persuade her fiancé to give up the inheritance altogether and find a job in the city of Huesca. His parents, on the other hand, implored him to stay on as the married head of the household; to sweeten the inheritance prospects they purchased the young couple a tractor as a wedding gift. The girl, however, remained adamant; she told her fiancé that they would either go to Huesca or there would be no marriage at all. To the chagrin of his family the boy acceded to her wishes and abandoned the household. He now works as a truck driver on a road construction crew and lives in Huesca. His wife is reported to be very happy in their modest city apartment.

The foregoing examples illustrate the strong desire, particularly on the part of the young, to live in terms of urban standards. Yet the same general desire is shared by a large part of the community. This is reflected in the considerable effort being made by villagers to import the conveniences and material goods of industrial civilization into the village. In the last fifteen years the greatest proportion of expenditures for the average family have gone toward improving material living conditions. Two decades ago such expenses composed only a small fraction of family budgets; nowadays Benabarre is on the road to becoming a genuine consumer society. There have been throughout the 1960s, for example, an endless series of house renovation projects. All the while I was in Benabarre numerous houses were undergoing reconstruction. At one time or another every village street was strewn with piles of sand, bricks, and debris where builders were engaged in some project. Many families had new gas kitchens installed; others built in modern bathrooms; still others had an entire floor converted into an independent apart-

*The building boom in Benabarre has made scenes such as this commonplace.*

ment. Various families had their whole dwellings demolished and rebuilt from the ground up. These completely renovated homes were always designed to conform as closely as possible to the new apartments being constructed in the cities. They have colored tile floors, brightly painted interiors, and are furnished with glossy cabinets and formica tables and chairs. A large number of these houses can now be seen on every main street of the community; their blue or white stucco facades stand in marked contrast to the older buildings.

Many homes are likewise being furnished with electrical appliances such as washing machines, refrigerators, electric mixers, and television sets. Most of these articles were rare in the village only ten or fifteen years ago. The first television set, for instance, appeared in Benabarre in 1960; in 1968 there were sixty homes which had them, and by 1971 the number had increased to ninety-four. The only item more significant than television as a symbol of urban affluence is the automobile. In the early 1950s there were less than ten cars in Benabarre. By 1968 the number had increased to fifty-two, and in 1971 there were more than one hundred.

The items mentioned are only a fraction of the panoply of industrial goods (from plastic hair curlers to detergents to bicycles) which villagers now purchase as a matter of course. Having such things is all part of the attempt, as villagers express it, to keep pace with *la vida moderna* (modern living). And the attempt is increasingly becoming a moral imperative; families which ignore these trends and continue to live according to the parsimonious standards of the past are exposed to the criticism of urban relatives and more "modern" villagers. They are told that they are "backward" or, even more harshly, that they "live like savages." Needless to say, these unprogressive households are having the greatest difficulty in persuading their sons to stay on in the household, or, having accomplished that, in finding them wives.

## THE NEW ECONOMY

The consumer economy just described would suggest that Benabarre is experiencing substantial material prosperity. Commodities such as automobiles, farm machinery, and television sets could not be purchased if Benabarrenses were not able to accumulate considerable cash savings. How, then, is this to be reconciled with the obvious instances of decline which have been documented in the bulk of this chapter? The statistics on emigration and the large number of moribund households certainly do not connote the most salutary economic conditions. These conditions are, however, only a part of a far more complex reality. There are also examples of unprecedented opportunities and economic growth in Benabarre which are as much a part of the local scene as are the abundant instances of decline.

This dual character of the village economy is in fact one of the most striking features of contemporary Benabarre. It also constitued one of the most perplexing problems of interpretation I faced when I began my work in the community. Depending upon whom I interviewed or conversed with, I alternated between the view that the village was in a serious state of decline, or contrariwise, that it was experiencing unprecedented growth. I eventually discovered, of course, that it was doing both, and that my conflicting impressions derived from the different social location of informants in the modernization process. When I spent time with persons who were fully a part of the commercial economy such as livestock dealers and entrepreneurial farmers, I was exposed to a highly optimistic view of the local situation. These individuals led me on tours of their modern pig or poultry farms and they typically brimmed with enthusiasm over their operations and plans for the future.

There were other days, however, which were spent principally in the company of the many peasant farmers in Benabarre whose futures in the community are decidedly unpromising. Such persons reflected a wholly pessimistic view of the community and its future. "All of this is coming to ruin" (*va a pique*, literally sinking) I was told too many times to remember; or, "Our sons all have to leave, there's no future for them here."

What I was witnessing was simply the differential impact of modernization, a characteristic of the process which has been remarked by a number of writers. As C. E. Black has expressed it (1966:27):

> ... the construction of a new way of life inevitably involves the destruction of the old. If one thinks of modernization as the integration or the reintegration of societies on the basis of new principles, one must also think of it as involving the disintegration of traditional societies.... Modernization must be thought of, then, as a process that is simultaneously creative and destructive, providing new opportunities and prospects at a high price in human dislocation and suffering.

These polar processes at work in Benabarre lend a highly dichotomous (even schizoid) quality to much of village life. The earlier economy and society is in utter disarray, while a new economy is being superimposed. There is always the possibility, therefore, that an observer may emphasize one of these realities at the expense of the other. This is, in fact, what is often done in the Spanish press. The country's newspapers and popular magazines reflect an overwhelmingly negative view of the changes occurring in the countryside; they emphasize breakdown and disintegration far more than what Black refers to the "creative" aspects of modernization. This often constitutes a serious distortion of what is actually taking place. In the remainder of this chapter I will briefly describe what can be termed the "regenerative" aspect of Benabarre's development.

Many of the same circumstances which are responsible for undermining the traditional economy have simultaneously opened up new opportunities. Thus the rapid expansion of the cities in relation to the countryside has meant that there is now an enormously increased demand for agricultural products from villages like Benabarre to sustain the growing urban population. Moreover, the development of efficient transportation, in the form of truck transport and improved highways, has greatly extended the effective hinterland upon which each city is able to draw for its products. Therefore, even though Benabarre is located at a considerable distance (some 190 kilometers) from Barcelona, it has become in the last few years a direct supplier of egg and meat products to the city.

This incorporation of the village within the orbit of city markets has resulted in a remarkable growth of commercial poultry and livestock farming. As the visitor enters Benabarre from any direction he sees evidence of the new industry. Large buildings which house pig or chicken farms have sprung up on the outskirts of the village, all having been built in the last ten years. They are all owned by villagers and many of them are gigantic enterprises compared to the modest scale of Benabarre's traditional agriculture. The largest of the pig farms are designed to hold as many as 1,500 pigs at once. One of Benabarre's poultry farmers maintains an output of 31,000 chickens fattened for market every three months. In the summer of 1971 there was another chicken farm being built which would eventually have the capacity for 45,000 birds. Egg farming has also become an important enterprise. There are eight households in Benabarre which maintain sizable operations. The largest of these is run by two families which recently pooled their resources to build a joint farm. They presently have 3,000 hens in continual output which produce some 175 dozen eggs per day. The production of other of Benabarre's egg farmers is nearly as great, so that every week trucks pick up hundreds of boxloads of eggs in Benabarre to be transported to Barcelona.

The rapid growth of the livestock industry is also related to mechanization. All of Benabarre's farmers have had a substantial portion of their labor time freed by the use of machinery. The same tasks which required hundreds of man hours when using draft animals or the scythe, are now accomplished in half a day with tractors and combines. This has made it possible for certain farmers to invest a great deal of time and energy into raising livestock.

Thus at least a part of Benabarre's agriculture has been transformed from household production to large-scale commercial operations. This trend will almost certainly continue in the future as Benabarre (like many Spanish villages) steadily becomes a kind of "rural food factory" (Halpern 1965:79) in order to meet the growing demand for agricultural products in the larger society.

The other major stimulus to the local economy, no less important than the livestock industry, has been the tourist trade. Its importance is also indicated by the large amount of new construction associated with it. Both within and outside of the village scores of summer homes (*chalets*) have been built to accommodate the growing numbers of people who come to spend vacations in Benabarre every summer. Those who come are city dwellers (most of them relatives of villagers) and since the early 1960s they have been buying deserted homes in the village to renovate them for use as summer cottages. Since 1967 a planned housing development (*urbanización*) has grown up adjacent to the village, entirely in the hands of village contractors. This "suburb" has grown very rapidly. I witnessed the first *chalet* being built in the summer of 1967, and three more in 1968. When I returned to the village in 1971 there were thirty complete homes and many more in the planning stages. Some villagers have built houses there, but the great majority are summer homes for urban visitors.

The investment in village property by urbanites represents a substantial infusion of capital into Benabarre as well as employment. The construction trades have been the single most dynamic sector of the village economy. In the early 1950s there were approximately twenty men in Benabarre employed full-time as *albañiles* (stonemasons). In 1971 there were sixty-one men who listed construction work

*The municipal swimming pool built to encourage summer tourism.*

as their principal occupation. The prosperity of many peasant households in Benabarre is related to the fact that their sons have been able to remain in the village and still bring in a good wage as full or part-time *albañiles*.

The willingness of urbanites to purchase property has also had a significant impact on property values. Deserted homes, once thought to be nearly worthless, are now in great demand, and outsiders often pay what villagers consider exorbitant prices for them. In 1971 a large house in the central plaza was being offered for sale; this house fifteen years ago was valued at about 50,000 *pesetas* ($833); in 1971 the owners were asking 500,000 *pesetas* ($7,140). Land values have also appreciated considerably; a parcel of land is presently worth between four and five times its value in the mid 1950s.

Thus all property owners are benefiting to some degree from the use of Benabarre as a summer resort. Certain families, however, have taken greater advantage of the situation than others. Approximately seventy families now rent out apartments to summer visitors. Many have converted an unused floor of their homes into modern apartments with kitchens. Others simply rent out extra rooms for the two months of July and August. This can yield a fair income; a family with two apartments to rent can earn as much as 22,000 *pesetas* ($313) in a summer.

The persons who have perhaps derived the greatest advantage from the tourist influx are the merchants. The population of Benabarre nearly doubles in summer and it is in this season that the shopkeepers make a large share of their yearly earnings. Merchants are also benefiting from the increased automobile and bus transit through the village. Bypass traffic now accounts for a significant percentage of sales in the grocery stores and in the four cafes and two restaurants. Therefore, even though the population of the village and of the surrounding region is declining, the number of effective consumers has increased notably. The automobile, along with the affluence of Spain's new middle classes, has made this expansion possible.

These various developments, coupled with the disintegration of the traditional economy, make Benabarre a specimen of the modernization process as it is occurring throughout rural Spain. In the next chapter I will trace out the major social implications of these events by means of an analysis of the changing patterns of stratification and prestige.

# 4/The changing class structure

In this chapter I want to draw out some of the social implications of the economic changes just described. It is a common observation among anthropologists that as economic forces are transformed, the social groupings or classes associated with these forces are variously affected. In Benabarre the economic revolution has occasioned the decline of certain social categories and the ascendancy of others. Through a description of these changes I hope to portray aspects of the new social order emerging in Benabarre and in large sections of rural Spain.

## SOCIAL LEVELING

Certainly the major social consequence of modernization in Benabarre has been the reduction of social differences. The institutional structure of hierarchy and inequality described in Chapter Two has been heavily eroded in the last two decades and is now virtually something of the past. There are no powerful patrons in the community, no clienteles, and the etiquette of interpersonal relations is predominantly egalitarian. Villagers think of the community as being composed mainly of social equals. As mentioned in the first chapter (pp. 16-17), when I first investigated the question of status in Benabarre most informants failed to acknowledge, or would not admit, that significant status differences existed. Furthermore, all contrasted the present situation with the stratified society of the prewar period. "Here everybody is about the same (*por un estilo*)"; or "Here everybody deals with everybody else by *tú*" (the familiar form of address); these were the most common modes of expressing this perceived equality.

Partial exceptions to this characterization were the few persons who could be considered modern representatives of the prewar bourgeoisie, such as the village priest, physician, and certain descendants of notable households. These were mentioned by various informants as having a legitimate claim to a degree of social superiority due to their education and family backgrounds. Informants often added, however, that these persons were such marginal members of the community (see pp. 66-68) that they could be left out of consideration altogether. It is unanimously agreed that the position of this stratum in the contemporary community bears little relationship to their exalted position a generation ago.

One thing is certain: there is far less distance between the ends of the social pyramid than was the case in the recent past. As villagers often express it, "The poor have gone up and the rich have come down." By and large this is an accurate assessment. The question to ask, then, is what forces have brought about this change? In order to answer the question I will first discuss the community's laboring population and then will have something to say about the bourgeoisie.

The greatest single force affecting the lower orders of village society has been the substantial rise in value of labor which has occurred in the last twenty years. Throughout Benabarre's history the lowest levels of the occupational and social hierarchy have been occupied by persons who labored for others. Included in this category were occupations such as day laborers (*jornaleros*), tenant farmers, shepherds, and servants. Like most of the villages in Spain, Benabarre has always been characterized by an overabundance of workers in relation to the demand for their services. Consequently, labor has commanded a low market value. It was this low value which formerly made it possible for wealthy landed families to employ large numbers of workers. Before the Civil War the largest landowner in Benabarre (Casa Abbad) had as many as fifteen workers at various times during the year, and all *señorito* families were able to surround themselves with servants.

Today such extravagant use of workers is out of the question. Labor value has appreciated to such an extent in the last two or three decades that now even the largest landowners cannot afford to employ more than one or two workers. The following table shows the average daily wage paid to agricultural laborers in Benabarre from 1935 to 1971.

| Year | Daily Wages (pesetas) |
|------|----------------------|
| 1935 | 5 |
| 1942 | 11 |
| 1945 | 22 |
| 1955 | 55 |
| 1960 | 90 |
| 1968 | 160 |
| 1971 | 225 |

The figures indicate that in thirty-six years the value of labor has increased forty-five times. While it is true that the greatest share of this increment is due to inflation, this is not the whole story; there has also been a definite improvement in the purchasing power of the daily wage. This can be demonstrated by comparing prices paid for foodstuffs in Benabarre in 1931 with the prices on the same items in 1968. The comparison yields a crude measure of the rise in cost of living as seen in the following table (p. 62).

If we calculate the average price differential in the two periods we find that prices have risen about twenty times over their value in 1931. This is considerably less than the rise in wages (thirty-two times between 1931 and 1968) which has taken place in the same period. There can be no doubt, therefore, that the purchasing power of labor has improved; this also accords with the fact that all village laborers maintain a standard of living which far exceeds the levels of 1931.

The explanation for this improvement is not far to seek: emigration to the

PRICES IN BENABARRE

|  | Sept. 1931 (pesetas) | Feb. 1968 (pesetas) |
|---|---|---|
| 300 gm codfish | .65 | 18.00 |
| ½ dozen eggs | 1.25 | 16.00 |
| 150 gm coffee | 1.20 | 24.00 |
| cond. milk (can) | 1.35 | 18.00 |
| 1 kg garbanzos | 2.00 | 35.00 |
| 200 gm cheese | 1.00 | 32.00 |
| 350 gm salt pork | 1.00 | 13.00 |
| sardines (can) | .60 | 15.00 |
| 1 liter cider | 2.25 | 12.00 |
| 300 gm biscuits | .90 | 21.00 |
| ¼ kg noodles | .65 | 5.00 |
| 100 gm almonds | .60 | 16.00 |
| 1 sack of rice | 1.15 | 22.00 |
| bleach (liter) | .50 | 4.00 |
| 1 chicken | 3.00 | 80.00 |
| 1 kg sugar | 1.60 | 16.00 |
| pimento (can) | .40 | 16.00 |

cities has considerably reduced Benabarre's pool of excess labor. As might be expected, a disproportionate number of emigrants from Benabarre have been those who own no property, particularly the supernumerary (non-heir) sons of peasant households. These were the persons who traditionally made up the bulk of the *jornalero* population. In the face of employment opportunities in the cities, which offer good wages and better living conditions than the village, emigration has been the most reasonable alternative for this class as a whole. The result has been a gradually increasing imbalance between the requirements for labor and its availability. By the mid 1960s Benabarre had become a labor-scarce community, particularly in the busy agricultural seasons. In the spring and early summer of 1968 I heard the constant lament from large and medium landowners that they could not find the workers they required. Elderly people often expressed amazement at the new situation. One remarked that when he was young it was the workers who had to beg for work. "Now it's all turned around. It's the owners who go looking for workers."

The shortage of workers has affected all economic activities which demand considerable labor. Landowners who depended on hired hands or sharecroppers to cultivate their fields have been forced to mechanize their operations. One conservative landowner told me that he resisted buying a tractor until a few years ago when he determined that paying three occasional farm hands was driving him steadily into the red. He then resolved to purchase a tractor, reduced his labor force to one man, and is now doing well. Sheepherding was, only a few years ago, one of the mainstays of the peasant economy. Many village households owned modest flocks, usually numbering no more than twenty animals. By 1968, however, all but a few households had abandoned sheepherding. The reason given was that they could not afford to pay shepherds the daily wage of two hundred *pesetas* which they demanded for guarding flocks. To afford a shepherd at such a wage, and con-

## THE CHANGING CLASS STRUCTURE

tinue to earn a profit, an owner had to maintain a minimum flock size of about one hundred animals. This is beyond the capital and pasture capacity of most farmers. Grape and wine production have met a similar fate. Proper maintenance of vineyards requires hired hands to weed and prune the vines and for the harvest. Labor costs have simply made small-scale production uneconomical; and between 1965 and 1971 most of Benabarre's farmers uprooted their vineyards to replace them with cereal crops.

Further evidence of the changed status of labor is the greatly reduced servant population. Although it is difficult to assemble accurate statistics on earlier periods, informants estimated that in the immediate prewar period there were between twenty-five and thirty household maids in Benabarre. In 1968 there were only four, and all were outsiders, hired from small hamlets in the mountain hinterland. But even these girls are becoming very difficult to find. Work as a maid is considered demeaning labor and there are now few households willing to send their daughters out to serve if there are alternatives. Even high wages are insufficient inducement for girls to hire on. In the spring of 1968 a family which runs a boardinghouse in Benabarre searched for a maid for three months; the one they eventually hired was virtually free to state her own terms of employment. Benabarre's mayor hired a maid at about the same time. On her first workday the girl informed the mayor's wife that she would not scrub the floors on her hands and knees; if they wanted the floors cleaned they would have to purchase her a mop. They did so the same afternoon.

The preceding discussion highlights the fact that the labor-scarce economy has placed unprecedented bargaining power in the hands of workers. The days are past when villagers were bound to an employer by his control over the only resources which could provide them a living. Villagers now have alternatives; if an employer makes onerous demands, or will not pay a just wage, his laborers seek employment elsewhere. The political implications of this new situation are not lost on villagers. As one informant stated:

> In the old days the *pobre* [poor person] couldn't speak up, he had to worry about his living. Now he can say whatever he wants. . . . In those days the *rico* [wealthy person] asked you to clean up the pig corral in his house and you thought you'd better do it, maybe without getting paid a thing. Now if somebody asks you to work you say, "Well, how much do you pay?"

The point of the above discussion is not to say that workers in Benabarre are highly paid or, by any stretch of the imagination, affluent. Those who are full-time workers continue to count among the poorest people of the community. The point is, however, that their poverty no longer impels them to become subservient to the wealthy. As anthropologists who have studied peasant villages in Japan have noted, the critical factor in determining whether or not patronage relations will arise seems to be "how poor are the poor" (Beardsley, et. al. 1959:274). Dependency relations and patron–clientage are most likely to appear under circumstances in which workers are little removed from a subsistence level. In such a situation it is expedient for the poor to depend on those who control life-giving resources. Where, on the other hand, workers have a clear margin beyond subsistence, servile relationships are far less common. This essentially explains what has occurred in

Benabarre. Those who sell their labor are poor but not wretchedly so; they are reasonably removed from a subsistence level and all have various alternatives in the expenditure of their labor. When villagers are asked, therefore, to state the main difference in the community between past and present they usually remark that people are more self-sufficient nowadays, and free of control by others. "Everybody lives independently," they say. "You don't have to link yourself (*ligarse*) to anyone now."

## THE RURAL BOURGEOISIE

The independence villagers speak of refers primarily to the fact that they are no longer bound by patronage obligations to the bourgeoisie. As suggested previously, this group is no longer the dominant stratum it was thirty years ago. The class has been reduced in both numbers and influence.

In 1971 there were nine families which could be considered the modern representatives of the prewar bourgeoisie. Three of the families are continuations of *señorito* households native to the village. The others are professionals or civil servants: the village priest, physician, lawyer, *secretario*, pharmacist, and a veterinary. The class is less than half the size it was a generation ago. The executions during the Civil War played a certain role in reducing their numbers. Those killed were almost all male heads of households, and some families were never able to recover from the loss. Certain family members simply did not return to Benabarre after the war; others, without the household head for support, were unable to maintain or pass on their positions.

Yet the main reason that so few of these families remain has been their disposition to emigrate. There is no longer an attempt on the part of such families to monopolize *carrera* positions in Benabarre. Recent economic development has so transformed the occupational structure of the country that there are now opportunities for *gente de carrera* outside of Benabarre which are more attractive than serving in a small village. Thus a number of successful sons of the old bourgeoisie still own property in the village but are presently lawyers, engineers, or doctors in the cities. The village has also lost many of its important civil servants. Benabarre's district court was removed some years ago to the city of Barbastro; therefore the community does not have a resident judge. And both Benabarre's judicial secretary and property registrar are absentee officials. They prefer to live in the nearby cities (where they can engage in subsidiary occupations) while their official duties are attended for them in Benabarre by caretaker clerks.

Benabarre is not atypical in this regard; throughout Huesca province virtually all the large villages have lost their native elites. In most of these villages and towns one can find deserted mansions which were once the residences of the bourgeoisie. Of course not all of the homes are deserted. Here and there one finds descendants still residing in the community. Yet where this is true it is generally the case that the position of the household has fallen significantly from what it was a generation ago. It often appears, in fact, that many of these households are in the hands of the least talented offspring. A son or daughter who received no education, or who never succeeded in gaining an independent career, has remained in the village to accept the inheritance. The phenomenon of decadent elites is so common in the region that there is a general phrase to describe them: *"los que no han sabido reaccionar"* (those who have been unable to adapt to the times).

A typical example is that of a bourgeois household in a community close to Benabarre. The household head, Francisco Perat, was one of four children. His eldest brother became a physician and now has a practice in a town near Valencia; Francisco's sister studied to become a schoolteacher but married a clothing merchant and lives in Barcelona; the other brother is an army officer. Francisco studied to become a notary but, despite various attempts, has never succeeded in passing the qualifying examinations. At an earlier point in his life he intended to remain in the village only until he could establish a position as notary in Zaragoza. Such hopes have waned now and he is resigned to remaining with his wife and children in the village. Although he has a great deal of land, he does not utilize it effectively, and does not engage personally in the agricultural labor. Other households in the village, although they own fewer resources, have been more successful in converting to modern agriculture. Francisco is regarded by other villagers as a rather ineffectual figure and is the butt of a good deal of concealed, but malicious, humor. When I mentioned this to the village priest the latter replied, rather regretfully:

> You see, many people in this village used to be their workers or servants. It now gives them a great deal of pleasure to see this family brought down to their own level.

The two most important notable families which remain in Benabarre are partial exceptions to the above characterization. They are exceptions to the extent that both have made a successful transition to large-scale, commercialized agriculture, and are well-off economically. They do, however, reflect the decline in position relative to the rest of the community which is characteristic of the class as a whole. No resident member of either family has a professional position, and the income of both households derives entirely from agriculture. Nor have they been able to maintain the marriage barrier between themselves and the rest of the community. Each of these households was left with female heiresses after the Civil War, both of whom married non-heir men from two of Benabarre's substantial landowning families. Their husbands' families are, however, *casas de labradores* (worker homes) with no claim to social distinction above the rest of the community. The marriages were considered below the station of the women, and villagers assured me that such matches would not have occurred in the past. The women are considered *gente fina* (refined people); both have been to the university and their education is far superior to that of their husbands. Yet it would have been difficult for either of them to find men of the same social position willing to live in Benabarre; the decision was either to emigrate, remain single, or marry down. Both women chose the latter alternative. In each case the man now resides in his wife's household.

The position of these two families has also changed in relation to their workers and dependents. Neither household controls anywhere near the labor force they were accustomed to employ in the past. The largest landowner (Casa Abbad) which once had as many as fifteen workers now employs two men on a steady basis and they retain a live-in cook. Not only has the number changed, but also the quality of relationship. Casa Abbad has had considerable turnover of personnel in recent years as various workers have departed for what they consider better employment in the cities. Their difficulties with workers was brought home to me by an incident which occurred during one of my visits to the household. I was engaged in conversation with the lady of the house and was puzzled by the fact that she frequently arose from her chair to peer out of the window. She finally confided that she was spying on one of their laborers who, she said, was loafing on the job. I asked why she did not say anything to him. She exclaimed, "Oh yes, and then he'll quit for sure and then where will we be?"

The labor situation is just one of the many ways in which the dominance of the former elite has diminished. I have dealt with it at length because it appears to be the single most important factor influencing interclass relations. Yet almost all criteria by which the bourgeoisie were formerly set apart have become less significant. It will be recalled that this class once held a near monopoly over the material symbols of urban civilization. Today, with great geographical mobility and the inundation of Benabarre by mass consumer goods, the ability to maintain this monopoly has vanished. As reported in the last chapter, many families have automobiles, television, and a wide range of material conveniences. There is, in fact, nothing of a material kind which bourgeois households possess which many other families cannot obtain as well. Nor is the bourgeoisie distinguished by an arena of exclusive participation such as the prewar *casino*. Benabarre has not had a *casino* since the Civil War and none of the cafes is restricted to any particular segment of the population.

The one quality by which the notables continue to be distinguished is their superior education. Yet even this difference is less than it was a generation ago. Education has been considerably democratized in Spain in the past twenty years, and secondary schooling has become accessible to a growing proportion of the population. In Benabarre approximately half of the adolescents now receive some post-primary education. In the last decade or so even farm households have produced children who have become teachers, lawyers, and white collar workers in the cities.

## SOCIAL WITHDRAWAL OF THE NOTABLES

The reduction of social differences within the community has had considerable impact on the public behavior of the bourgeoisie. There has been a marked tendency in the past decade for the remaining members of this class to draw a curtain of isolation between themselves and the rest of the community. This applies particularly to the native families, but also to the professionals and civil servants. Their homes, which were once centers of social activity, are now insular premises which other villagers rarely penetrate. Members of this stratum do not maintain close social contacts with other villagers and they participate minimally in the public life of the community.

I became aware of the degree to which the bourgeoisie were set apart from others when I made my first attempts to become acquainted with Benabarre's important old families. On these occasions my normal procedure of having one informant introduce me to others brought poor results. When I asked friends if they could put me in contact with one or another of the notable families they excused themselves saying that they had little relationship (*relación*), or they did not deal socially (*alternar*), with the family in question. Some suggested it would be better if the schoolmaster or some other influential person would take me to their homes. This was unlike my experience in meeting any other villager; until that point in my fieldwork it had appeared that any resident could introduce me to any other individual in Benabarre. It was clear that this did not apply to the notable families; intimate social ties apparently linked them to very few persons in Benabarre.

This isolation was most pronounced among the native landholding families. One of the most important of these resides in a villa two kilometers above the village. Members of the family rarely descend to Benabarre except to pick up household supplies or for an occasional religious celebration. Nor do they socialize with other families of the community. They told me that before the Civil War there were a number of close friends of the family living in Benabarre whom they visited frequently. But now, they say, there are so few persons of their social status in the community that they have little incentive to visit.[1] It is apparent that this family regards Benabarre as a wholly "plebeian" village now that it no longer contains the stratum of important personages who once lent it distinction.

The other prominent *señorito* family is similarly withdrawn. The male head of the household is from the ranks of the ordinary villagers and has maintained many of his former associations. Other members of the family, however, keep their distance. The only persons in Benabarre with whom the heiress and her elderly mother have regular social contact are the village schoolmaster and his family. And except for very faithful attendance at church, both women tend to remain in the seclusion of their home. The heiress has even isolated her thirteen year old daughter from other village children to such an extent that the girl has virtually no friends or associations within Benabarre. Recreation and social life for this family consists in visiting relatives in the nearby towns, and in receiving them as guests in summer.

This exclusiveness on the part of the bourgeoisie is recognized by villagers as a relatively new phenomenon. Many of my elderly informants who were once intimately associated with certain of these families typically have no association with the same household today. Some have been deeply offended by the changed relationship. One elderly peasant who grew up as a *criado* in one of the notable households complained that he is no longer welcome there. He remarked, "Now if you go to that house you have to state your business right away, and if you don't have any business you'll be sent on your way."

---

[1] The remaining members of the bourgeoisie rarely socialize among themselves. The main reason seems to be that they either dislike or are jealous of one another.

The changed public behavior of the bourgeoisie is closely related to what I will refer to as the new "status ambiguity" in Benabarre. The upward mobility of the lower orders of village society, especially in relation to the weakened status of the notables, has lessened the security of position for everyone. In the past, most interclass interaction took place within the framework of patronage in which the notables treated others as dependents. Today, for all but the most humble villagers, dependency relations with the elite are no longer appropriate. Few villagers depend on the notables economically and none wants to think of himself as a recipient of their charity. The notables, for their part, must be sensitive to the villagers' new conception of self-reliance. The potential delicacy of interclass relations is illustrated by the comment of a lady of one of the elite households. She told me that it was formerly their custom to distribute their used clothing among Benabarre's poor families, but they have recently discontinued the practice for fear of committing an indiscretion. "Nowadays," she stated, "I prefer to throw away a perfectly good sweater rather than risk offending somebody by offering it."

Today, therefore, interaction with others does not necessarily reaffirm the superiority of the notables. It may, on the contrary, suggest a situation of practical equality. For example, some of Benabarre's young men, infused by the spirit of egalitarianism common to large portions of Spanish youth, are reluctant to acknowledge certain status differences which have been traditionally accepted in the community. A few of them told me that they use the familiar form of address (*tú* —implying equality) with everyone of their generation in Benabarre. Since the village physician is of approximately the same age, they also address him familiarly. The doctor has never objected, but it was evident to me that he considered their behavior presumptuous. In one of our conversations he disclaimed friendship with any of them and referred disparagingly to this group as *paletos* (derogatory term for peasant, meaning "yokels").

The voluntary withdrawal and social isolation of the notables can be seen, in part, as a means of protecting their position in a situation in which many of the former distinctions between themselves and others have disappeared. Maintenance of the social gulf has become an important means of differentiating themselves from elements of a society which have approximated their position in a number of ways. In a situation in which there was no ambiguity concerning the exalted position of one stratum over another, where each knew his place, there was no particular threat to the elite in intimate contact with persons they considered their inferiors. The easygoing familiarity between elite and peasant in Benabarre was always a function of this conception of hierarchy. But now that all social relationships have taken on a more egalitarian cast, personal intimacy begins to imply social equality; as such it becomes a threat to the notables' claim to superiority. Benabarre's former elite has therefore begun to behave like the upper classes in more egalitarian societies, where (as, for instance, in the United States) residential segregation and degrees of interpersonal association become important indicators of social position.[2]

---

[2] For elaboration of this argument see my article in *Ethnology*, Vol. XI, No. 4, pp. 386-98, October, 1972.

## THE NEW MIDDLE CLASS

Admittedly the foregoing discussion of the bourgeoisie is somewhat out of proportion to their importance in the community. It should be evident that, given their withdrawal, they no longer play a very significant role in Benabarre. Yet the discussion has served to convey two important points: that the traditional division of the community between *señoritos* and other villagers has been overcome; and that the society is now far more egalitarian than it ever was in the past.

I now turn to discuss the social stratum, or class, which has become increasingly prominent in Benabarre since the Civil War and has essentially replaced the bourgeoisie as the dominant element in the village. I will refer to this group as the "new middle class." The term is not entirely satisfactory since the group is definitely an upper stratum in Benabarre. Yet for two significant reasons the term middle class seems more appropriate. First, most members of the stratum are associated with commerce or entrepreneurship; and second, their aspirations, associations, and pattern of living all relate them to the growing middle classes of the surrounding towns and cities.

The stratum is composed of approximately forty families, almost all of whom are part of the urban–industrial economy which has penetrated Benabarre in the last twenty years. Member households include successful merchants, livestock dealers, entrepreneurial farmers, and a few petty officials. The fact that merchants are found in this category is nothing new; the owners of sizable commercial establishments have always been an important grouping in the community and continue to be so today. The livestock dealers and capitalized farmers, however, are manifestations of the new economy, their existence made possible by innovations in agriculture which have occurred in the past twenty years. Most of the latter therefore represent considerable social mobility. In particular they form a dramatic contrast to the majority of farmers in Benabarre from whom they have become differentiated.

Benabarre's new middle class is set apart by three main criteria: their political importance, the economic well-being of its members, and by relative modernism. The political ascendancy of this stratum began shortly after the Civil War. The wartime executions temporarily eliminated Benabarre's prewar elite leaving positions of community influence open to others. Those who eventually filled the positions were from the ranks of the "ordinary" villagers. None had professional careers or education; they were either of merchant families or were farmers with very large patrimonies. As one of these men expressed it, "With the important men gone it was left to us to run the village."

This statement is accurate in the sense that in the past thirty years almost all local governmental positions have been held by members of this stratum. During all but four of these years the mayorship has been occupied by either merchants or farmer–businessmen. The six councillor positions in the *ayuntamiento* are also perpetually rotated among storeowners, livestock dealers, and salaried state employees. It would be inaccurate, however, to foster the impression that these men are either very powerful, or that they are strongly motivated politically.

Since the Civil War Spain has had a rigidly centralized political system which has assimilated unto itself many of the power resources which were formerly controlled locally. This centralization has had the effect of markedly reducing the level of meaningful political activity in Benabarre. Residents do not choose their village officials—except for inconsequential elections held for two of the six councillor positions. The mayor and *secretario* are appointed by higher authorities in the cities. There are no active political parties, no campaigns, and few overt political events of any kind. Even many decisions on matters of importance to the village are made by administrators in Huesca. It is this centralized control, and power of administration, which lies behind the boast of spokesmen for the national regime that it has eliminated *caciquismo* (boss rule) in the villages. That *caciquismo* has been reduced in Benabarre, and in all the villages I observed, there can be little doubt. It is equally true, however, that this centralization has engendered a remarkably barren political environment throughout rural Spain.

Thus the fact that the middle class dominates village government should not imply that they wield a great deal of power, or that the rest of the village is at their mercy. Political apathy runs high in Benabarre and few villagers are anxious to accept official positions, even those as innocuous as village councillor. And although these appointments cannot be legally refused, there are cases of villagers who have done so. When I interviewed members of the village government almost every one made efforts to convince me that he had not actively sought his position but had accepted it upon the insistence of others, and then only reluctantly as a means of serving the community.

The middle class is also distinguished by relative affluence. They are the owners of the businesses or enterprises which serve the modern economy, especially the livestock industry, merchandising, and the tourist trade. They therefore possess considerable liquid wealth. In 1967-1968 certain of Benabarre's merchants and livestock dealers had annual incomes in excess of 300,000 *pesetas* ($4,285). This can be compared to a figure of between 65,000 and 80,000 *pesetas* ($928 to $1,143) for the average village household. Income, however, should not be confused with total worth. There are other residents, certain farm families for example, which own more valuable property (in buildings and land) than various middle class families. Nevertheless, fixed wealth of this kind does not enable them to participate in the consumer economy to the same degree as the middle class. The homes of the latter are usually better furnished with amenities and conveniences, they usually have automobiles, and they are also the persons most committed to—and best able to afford—secondary education for their children.

The class is not a cohesive group in the sense that they often work in concert; yet there is a degree of unity which derives from viewing themselves as progressive people as contrasted to other villagers (perhaps a majority) whom they tend to regard as backward (*atrasado*). It is, in fact, this criterion of relative modernism which is probably the single most important characteristic in differentiating them from others. I can best illustrate my meaning by an incident which occurred in the summer of 1967.

At that time the most important project of the village government was to build a community swimming pool (to encourage summer tourism) by means of community and state funds. But when costs outran the available financing, the *secre-*

*tario* decided to call for voluntary contributions from villagers. Before inviting all residents, however, he called a meeting of the heads of approximately fifty households to discuss the project and to secure their financial support. These were essentially members of the stratum I am considering here, plus some of the wealthy tradesmen. Two weeks later a call was issued to all heads of households in the community. When I later asked the *secretario* on what basis he had chosen the original group he replied that they were the "forward looking" members of the community. He added that he felt that if he could get this group to support the project it would have a good chance of success; if not, then there could be little expectation that others would do so.

The section of the middle class which best typifies this progressivism are the entrepreneurial farmers, about twenty households in all. These are men who have been successful in the last fifteen years in the livestock trade or in large-scale mechanized farming. A few are owners of properties which were either originally large, or they have been able to expand their hectarage by reclaiming lands from the forests. These large properties have benefited most from the introduction of machinery and the owners have generally devoted the land to large-scale cereal production.

But the majority of the entrepreneurial farmers are individuals who have entered some aspect of the livestock trade or poultry farming; they are owners of the large enterprises mentioned in the preceding chapter (p. 57). The characteristics of this group which set them apart from other farmers in Benabarre are their willingness to innovate and to risk substantial capital investment in their enterprise. Agriculture for them has become a business in the strict sense of the term. They apply scientific methods to their operations as well as cost-accounting business procedures. They are also self-consciously aware of the difference between themselves and the rest of the peasant population. As one of them told me:

> Today you have to do everything modern, up-to-date. Farming like our fathers did it is a dead end. That's what's wrong with most of the farmers of this village, they're not progressive.

Some examples will illustrate the nature of their operations. Ramón Vivas is the individual who introduced commercial egg farming into Benabarre. He was of a peasant household which until the mid 1950s was undistinguished from others. In 1949 he read an article in an agricultural magazine which deplored the low production of eggs in Spain as compared to France; the article went on to point up the tremendous internal egg market for Spanish farmers. This was his original stimulus and he decided to explore the possibilities in egg farming. Through friends of his family he was introduced to a poultry expert in the city of Lérida. This gentleman undertook to explain in detail how Ramón should proceed, and presented him with a gift of twelve hens to get him started. Ramón's profits were substantial from the beginning, and throughout the 1950s he plowed the best part of his earnings into expanded operations. He began subscribing to a professional journal on *avicultura* (care of poultry) and used it as a guide to found his system on a firm scientific basis. He now vaccinates his birds regularly; mixes his own feeds and additives; keeps each hen in an individual cage so that it will expend

*Taking in the harvest, as it is done by Benabarre's new middle class.*

its energy in laying eggs rather than in aimless exercise; he keeps close tabs on each hen so that he can remove the nonproducers to sell for meat; and he uses electric lighting to extend the waking hours of the hens to maximize daily output. He also maintains double-entry bookkeeping and knows the exact margin of profit he can expect at any given egg-price level. Ramón has been very successful and a number of others have imitated him, both in Benabarre and in the surrounding villages.

The owners of the commercial pig and poultry farms (chickens raised for meat rather than for eggs) maintain equally sophisticated operations. Many of these farms were initially built with the aid of state loans, but most owners are now out of debt and are able to expand operations on the basis of reinvested earnings. One of the poultry farms I toured in the summer of 1971 is almost entirely automated and requires only two laborers (one for the day shift and another for night) to oversee the 31,000 birds. The feed is delivered to the chickens on a conveyor belt from the grain silo; the temperature is constantly regulated; the farm is sprayed for insects daily, and the owner boasted to me that I would not find one fly on the premises. To guard against contamination each person entering the farm must chemically disinfect his shoes. The chickens are fed a high potency diet of grains and vitamins which fattens them in the shortest possible time. The farm is even equipped with blue electric lights (which give visibility but which suggest darkness to the chickens) so the birds will not stampede when they are loaded at night into trucks for shipment to Barcelona. The owner, like all of Benabarre's pig and poultry farmers, has carefully geared his operations to the demands of the urban

## THE CHANGING CLASS STRUCTURE

market. He is aware of normal seasonal gluts and shortages and attempts to plan his production to peak at periods when prices can be expected to be most favorable.

All of these farmers appreciate the need to continually expand operations. The competition from new farms being built throughout the region has steadily lowered prices and lessened the profit margin on all agricultural products. Benabarre's entrepreneurs have been forced to expand to remain competitive. When I returned to Benabarre in 1971 after a three year absence I found that nearly all of the modern farmers had increased their scale of operations. One who was in the process of enlarging his farm expressed the state of the economy when he remarked, "Nowadays, to stay the same size means going backwards. I have to expand even if I only want to earn what I'm earning now."

These examples give an idea of the extent to which the farmer–entrepreneurs are part and parcel of the modern economy. They also illustrate some of the complex business and intellectual skills which have been essential for success. And since this group represents a small minority of the total farming population, it is intriguing to ask what personal qualities they share which appear to have been instrumental in their rise above their peers. The group is heterogeneous so there are not a great many qualities common to all of them. Some, however, are worthy of mention.

Firstly, all of the entrepreneurs are young men, or at least they were young (in their twenties or early thirties) when they first began to distinguish themselves. Another common characteristic is that, as a group, they have traveled more than

*A section of one of Benabarre's automated chicken farms which contains some 31,000 birds.*

others and have observed developments in other areas of Spain. Certainly all of the pig and poultry farmers have deliberately modeled their operations on prototypes they have observed elsewhere, particularly in Catalonia. Formal education has *not* been a factor. None of the farmer–entrepreneurs has had significantly more formal schooling than other members of his generation. Given the nature of the Spanish educational system, with its humanistic and literary bias, this is not unexpected; Spaniards with secondary education are extremely reluctant to employ their talents in agriculture. Finally, most of the entrepreneurs have not come from strictly peasant backgrounds. Only three of the truly innovative farmers (of which Ramón Vivas is one) have been heirs to family patrimonies. The large majority have been either supernumary sons of farm households or individuals with prior experience in commerce, or some other nonagricultural occupation (carpenter, miller, transporter, etc.). It would appear that certain peasant characteristics, such as caution and provincialism, have made it more difficult for peasants than for others to react constructively to the new opportunities.

## THE TRADITIONAL FARMERS

The majority of Benabarre's farmers form a sharp contrast to the entrepreneurs discussed above. Whereas the latter have been upwardly mobile in the last two decades, the households I will refer to as "traditional" farmers have experienced an overall decline in social status. Thus Benabarre's agricultural population is now divided in an unprecedented way. In the past the major difference among the peasants was simply between those with large amounts of land and those with less. In the contemporary community this difference has become subordinate to the distinction between modern entrepreneurs and those who remain attached to the subsistence economy. Or, expressed in a slightly different manner, the farm population has become increasingly divided into a modern and traditional sector.

By "traditional" farmers I mean all of those agriculturists who have continued working approximately the same family patrimony as the preceding generation. Their distinguishing characteristic is that they have done almost nothing new; they have not developed large-scale livestock, poultry, or cereal production. In the present dynamic state of the economy this has meant stagnation and decline. As one farmer expressed it, "If a peasant in this village has not set out in new directions (*si no ha cogido una rama nueva*) he is going downhill." Approximately 70 percent of Benabarre's farmers (and more than one-fourth of the village population) can be included in this category.

As pointed out in the last chapter, many of these are elderly. Most of them began farming in Benabarre long before there was any possibility of developing the highly capitalized, scientific farming described in the preceding section. Their attitudes toward agriculture are therefore those associated with the earlier economy in which the basic aim was to provision a household, rather than to develop a genuinely commercial enterprise. Their basic strategy of production is to maintain operating costs at a minimum. Until recently some even resisted making necessary investments in chemical fertilizers, hybrid seed, and equilibrated feeds for live-

*A "traditional" farmer plowing the fields as it has been done for centuries.*

stock. As a result, there have often been considerable differences in production between these households and others. In 1968 the per hectare wheat yield of some of the conservative peasants was only half that obtained by many of Benabarre's younger farmers who had learned the value of fertilization and the use of new hybrid seed.

It is obvious that conservatism and outmoded attitudes have prevented these elderly farmers from capitalizing on new opportunities. There are other peasants in the "traditional" category, however, who cannot be considered backward to the same degree. For these it is much less their conservatism which has prevented them from becoming part of the modern economy as it has been shortage of capital and lack of scientific or commercial skills. It must be recognized that the attempt to enter the arena of commercialized farming is fraught with risk. Even Benabarre's most successful poultry and livestock farmers have faced numerous crises and setbacks as they built up their operations. And there are various examples in Benabarre of persons who have attempted to become poultry or egg farmers and have failed. When, for instance, it became apparent that Ramón Vivas had achieved success as an egg farmer, a large number of families attempted to do likewise. Around 1960 there was even what informants describe as a chicken farm "craze" in Benabarre. Various households made substantial investments in chickens and equipment and converted the upper floors of their homes into small chicken farms. But then, within a year or two, most of them gave up the attempt after incurring considerable losses. Some failed because they had insufficient capital; they could not establish the business on the necessary scale; nor could they weather the various periods of market gluts when egg prices were unfavorable to the farmer. Others were lax about vaccinating their hens and then lost them to disease. Still others failed to establish the bookkeeping techniques which would have informed them of the exact point at which they were operating at a profit or at a loss.

The difficulty of entering the modern sector has meant that the farming of most peasants has remained on the diminutive scale of household production. For these peasants farming does not provide a great deal beyond household necessities. Some cash income is produced from the sale of almonds and of excess cereal production. They also breed pigs to sell the litters to Benabarre's livestock dealers. For most households, however, an approximately equal amount of cash income is now obtained from part-time labor: as construction workers, as occasional farm hands, or the wife does sewing piecework in the home, and there are additional labor possibilities. It is only by virtue of becoming part-time workers that such families have been able to participate to any extent in the consumer economy.

Thus in terms of general socio-economic condition, there is now little to distinguish Benabarre's traditional peasants from the landless laborers. This was not the case in the recent past. Formerly possession of land was a major determinant of social position, and was sufficient to give the peasants a status in the community considerably above that of the *jornaleros*. But the change from a subsistence economy to the present money economy has materially lessened the importance of land. In a subsistence economy land is crucial; it provides most of life's necessities, the main concern of nearly everyone. In a consumer economy, on the other hand, land is valuable mainly as a factor of production; the concern is with the amount of money income it produces. This, of course, is its great failing today; the annual income produced by a fifteen hectare farm may be even less than that earned by a full-time road construction employee or a worker in the building trades. It is for considerations such as these that the peasants are being drawn into the labor market, and the reason that many have given up farming altogether to become permanent workers.

## THE SKILLED TRADES

The only important occupational group not yet discussed is that of the members of the skilled trades. These are referred to locally as men with *oficio* (trade, skill). Included in the group are those occupations which require some special training or apprenticeship, such as carpenter, mason, plumber, mechanic, barber, baker, and so forth. Except for a few village craftsmen whose livelihoods have been undermined by manufactured goods, the skilled tradesmen have benefited from modernization. The building boom in Benabarre has augmented the need for specialized services of masons, carpenters, electricians, and plumbers. And the investment in higher living standards has increased the dependence on mechanics, barbers, tailors, and bakers. Most of Benabarre's tradesmen have more work than they can handle and the demand for their services has occasioned an enormous rise in the cost of skilled labor. In 1968, for example, Benabarre's master masons were earning approximately 350 *pesetas* ($5.00) per day; only three years later, in the summer of 1971, their daily wage had nearly doubled to 650 *pesetas* ($9.30). As might be expected, villagers express a great deal of dissatisfaction over these rising wages. One man told me angrily that the builders (*albañiles*) are the new *caciques* ("exploiters" in this context) of Benabarre because, "They charge whatever they want and people just have to pay."

The relationship between modernization and the prosperity of the skilled trades is best demonstrated by a comparison of tradesmen in some of the smaller villages of the region with their counterparts in Benabarre. In the smaller and more remote communities there has been far less construction, or modernization of living patterns than has occurred in larger villages like Benabarre. In the former communities masons and carpenters earn only slightly better than half the daily wages earned by their counterparts in Benabarre. And tradesmen in these villages are in about the same general socio-economic status as smallhold peasants.

In Benabarre, on the contrary, skilled tradesmen have surpassed the traditional peasants economically and have effectively replaced them in the upper half of the community's status hierarchy. In fact, some of the wealthiest tradesmen, particularly the builders, can be considered marginal members of the new middle class. The tradesmen were in far more humble circumstances a generation ago. One of the master masons remembers that in his adolescence he courted a girl from one of the community's medium peasant households. The courtship ended when the girl's father told him bluntly that he was too poor to have a chance with his daughter. The mason added, with some satisfaction, "That same family would give anything if my daughter would take an interest in their son today."

The example of the skilled trades serves to underline the theme stressed throughout this chapter: that the penetration of the commercial–industrial economy has restructured the community both economically and socially. And while this penetration has annulled certain social differences, others are in the process of creation. It remains for the future to determine what will become of the modern–traditional distinction. Yet my guess is that it will gradually fade in importance. I say this because Benabarre's traditional sector is not reproducing itself; the sons and daughters of these households are rapidly departing for the cities.

This brings us to the subject of the following chapter: the relationships between villagers and the urban world beyond.

# 5 / The village and the outside world

No analysis of modernization in Benabarre would be complete without reference to the changes taking place in the relationship between the community and the larger society. On numerous occasions I have mentioned that industrial technology and the new communications have bound the village more firmly within the orbit of national–metropolitan Spain. The impact of technology is, however, only one aspect of the new integration; there is an important social dimension as well. An extensive network of personal ties has grown up in recent years which link individuals in Benabarre to numerous families in the surrounding towns and cities. In the following sections I will describe these relationships, and then will attempt to point up some of the political significance of these linkages for the community as a whole. Finally, I will have something to say about the institutional connections which relate Benabarre to the larger society.

## CITY–VILLAGE SOCIAL TIES

It should be apparent at this point that the world of the cities has become increasingly significant for the average villager. Urban influences have invaded Benabarre at a remarkable pace in the last few years. Even more importantly, villagers find themselves reaching out to the metropolitan areas for numerous services which were irrelevant, or even nonexistent, in the recent past. Examples of such services abound. Parents, for instance, who are concerned with providing secondary education for their children must secure their admission to the appropriate schools in the cities; they must also find places for the students to live. Villagers who have become members of medical insurance programs, or who are beneficiaries of social security, make regular use of clinics in Lérida and Huesca. Serious ailments, dental problems, operations, and child deliveries, all are now routinely handled in the cities. Benabarre's pig and poultry farmers deal with middlemen who purchase their produce; and the community's shopkeepers maintain enduring relationships with urban suppliers. The cities are also seats of governmental power where dealings with bureaucracy must be managed. Matters as diverse as securing business permits, having social security papers signed, or obtaining a driver's license—all may occasion visits to agencies in the provincial capital.

Few of these metropolitan connections were significant a generation ago. It is only in the last fifteen years that ordinary villagers have attempted to educate their children beyond the village school; there was no social security program in the past; villagers were formerly reluctant to deal directly with governmental agencies, and they made use of urban medical services only in cases of extreme emergency.

As Benabarrenses have made progressively greater use of urban facilities, there has been a corresponding increase in both the number and quality of social relations maintained with persons living in metropolitan areas. It will be recalled (pp. 35-36) that in the prewar era only the bourgeoisie had effective social ties in the society beyond the village. Social life for ordinary villagers centered on the local region, and they tended to look upon the cities as something of an alien world. Such an attitude is still reflected in the behavior of Benabarre's elderly folk. They are generally ill at ease in the cities; they express a dislike of the noise and bustle there and lack confidence in their ability to handle even simple tasks such as boarding streetcars or entering a strange cafe. One old man who now visits his daughter in Barcelona about once every year, told me that he hates the city because he gets lost as soon as he leaves his daughter's apartment. "All those streets and buildings look just the same," he complained. The present adult generation and Benabarre's young people are very different in this regard. They are more at ease in the cities and their behavior and frankly expressed opinions indicate that most of them find the urban milieu exhilarating.

Various elements have combined to bring about this change in the generations. The approximation in culture between urban and rural areas, due partly to an all-embracing material culture, has made many characteristics of city life familiar realities. Television and popular magazines transmit images of the metropolitan world continually; and the ease of travel allows villagers to visit the cities with much greater frequency than did their parents. Yet the element which has been most influential in bringing the cities closer to villagers has been the remarkable "personalization" of city life which has occurred in the last twenty years. To a large extent this personalization is a by-product of the massive emigration from the village.

As noted earlier, most emigration from Benabarre has not been of entire families, but rather of children of households which continue in the community. The result is that a large proportion of individuals have immediate relatives—a child, a brother, or sister—who live and work in the surrounding towns and cities. And even if an individual does not have immediate kin in these areas, he is certain to have friends and acquaintances. There is hardly a city in the region which does not contain some people from Benabarre or from the local area. Villagers even make the joking comment about Barcelona that "There are more Benabarrenses in Barcelona than there are in Benabarre."

I was struck by the apparently large number of urban acquaintances of my village friends the first time they accompanied me to the city of Lérida. The female passengers bore baskets of garden vegetables, spiced sausages, and wine for relatives and friends they intended to visit. As we entered the city, and drove along the streets, my companions maintained an almost ceaseless commentary on the whereabouts of former villagers. One pointed to an apartment complex saying that a girl

*Summer visitors from Barcelona in one of the village stores.*

of such-and-such a household lived there with her husband; another indicated a garage where the son of one of Benabarre's carpenters was employed as a mechanic; a woman pointed to a shoestore where her cousin worked, and so on.

The social connection between village and city is, however, by no means confined to visits by villagers to the cities. There is an equal, or perhaps greater, flow in the opposite direction. As noted previously, urban relatives come to Benabarre in large numbers for summer vacations and for special holidays such as Christmas and the Lenten season. Virtually every family in Benabarre receives urban relatives on one or more of these occasions. Not all of the vacationers are relatives, but the majority are. They, or their parents, are *hijos del pueblo* (sons of the village) who emigrated some years earlier. They now return to Benabarre to visit their elderly parents or brothers and sisters, and to spend a tranquil vacation in the village.

The large-scale vacationing as practiced today is a recent phenomenon. Only since the 1960s have visitors begun to come to Benabarre in appreciable numbers. Prior to the Civil War a handful of urban bourgeois families used to spend summers in the community, but these represented a small number of visitors. Travel was a luxury then, and only relatively wealthy families were able to afford a vacation of that kind. Since the late 1950s the situation has changed markedly. The rising standards of living of Spain's lower middle classes have opened up to them new avenues for recreation and travel. Many own automobiles and urban business establishments typically grant their employees a full month's vacation in summer. Spending the interlude in their native village is inexpensive and offers them the pleasure of renewing ties with kinsmen and friends.

I should point out that Benabarre is not exceptional in this regard. It is a growing practice throughout Spain for urban residents to desert the cities every summer in favor of highland or coastal villages. The custom is referred to everywhere in Spain as *el veraneo*. Anthropologists who have studied mountain villages in Andalusia (Pitt-Rivers 1954:80) and in Castile (Kenny 1961:42-43; Aceves 1971:117) report a pattern of summer visiting almost identical to that found in Benabarre.

The entire atmosphere of Benabarre changes at this time. The level of general social activity is greater than at any other period of the year. In the afternoons the central plaza is filled with mothers watching children and conversing. Small children and adolescents ride their bicycles or play various games. There are groups of old men in casual conversation while others are immersed in card matches, or they simply observe others. The cafes are crowded and all the stores do a brisk business. On various evenings of the week there are dances for the teen-agers. Villagers are unanimous in the opinion that summer is the prime season of the year, and they lament the fact that Benabarre does not have a similar level of *animación* at other times. The contrast between this season and the long winter, when villagers are left to themselves, is a sharp one. I once had the experience of driving a resident of Zaragoza up to Benabarre in late November. He normally visits the village only in summer, but my offer of a ride induced him to visit some friends in Benabarre. He seemed shocked as we drove into the cold and deserted central plaza, which he is accustomed to see filled with people. He shook his head slowly and exclaimed, "¡Qué triste está Benabarre!" (How sad Benabarre is!).

Another link in the chain of relationships between residents and city relatives is observable during the months of December and January. At this time hundreds of packages and parcels are sent out from Benabarre to relatives in the cities. They contain the products of the *matanza* (slaughter of the household pig) such as *tortetas* (made from pork fat, sugar and spices, and shaped like a doughnut); *patas* (pig's feet) and *longaniza* (spiced sausages). All are items which urbanites are delighted to receive from the country, particularly when prepared in the style and taste of their native village.

## URBAN–RURAL RECIPROCITY

The ties I have adumbrated can be thought of, at least analytically, as a species of "exchange" relationship: villagers provide certain rural products and hospitality, while urbanites accommodate villagers when something is required from the world of the cities. Before proceeding to a description of this interchange, however, I should point out that villagers do not think of the relationships in these utilitarian terms. From their point of view the ties are simply based on the natural affection between kinsmen and friends; and the suggestion that they use each other as means to other ends would undoubtedly be offensive. It is necessary to emphasize, therefore, that my point here is not that instrumentality is the necessary basis of these relationships, but simply that it is a sociologically important consequence of them. To prove otherwise I would have to show that villagers consistently slough off, and forget, those relatives which are not useful; and I have little evidence to support such a position. Nevertheless, the fact remains that these ties play an important part in the orientation of villagers to the society beyond the village, and it is this very practical aspect of the relationships with which I am mainly concerned.

The principle upon which the exchange is based is that of reciprocity: a person does a favor for a kinsman or friend secure in the knowledge that he will be treated similarly in the future. The concept of general reciprocity is an important social mechanism in Benabarre, as it is in Spain generally. I discovered repeatedly in my dealings with villagers that when I did simple favors they made prompt efforts to reciprocate. My gift of a few pencils and erasers to some children brought the girls back the following day bearing me a dozen eggs—sent of course from their parents. After giving a villager a ride to Lérida I was often invited for a meal in his home, or he offered his services as an informant, and I could cite numerous similar examples. The important point is that this did not occur occasionally or sporadically, but with almost perfect regularity. I soon came to expect such behavior and became self-conscious about what villagers expected of me along similar lines.

A comparable reciprocity mechanism operates in all dealings between villagers and their urban relatives and friends. The relationships are highly informal and there is little effort to balance out accounts. One party is the dispenser of favors now, and will be the recipient of them at another time and place. The general expectation prevails that over the long term both parties will give and receive approximately equally. But even if this is not the case the relationships do not necessarily break down.

The major contribution of villagers is the hospitality they offer in summer and on important holidays. Most of the relatives who vacation in Benabarre reside with village families, usually staying in the natal households in which they were raised. Village homes are spacious; almost all were built to accommodate larger families than those which inhabit them today.[1] Thus extra rooms are converted into sleeping quarters for visiting families. As long as the relatives remain they are treated as guests; with very few exceptions the costs of their food and lodgings are borne by villagers. The occasional exceptions occur when, for example, a large urban family descends on a peasant household. In such an instance the woman of the former may accept responsibility for purchasing groceries and the like. But such circumstances are uncommon; in the vast majority of cases villagers extend hospitality and provide everything required. This can run into considerable expense if the guests stay for a long period. I occasionally heard disgruntled comments about relatives whom villagers considered had overstayed their welcome. As one informant remarked, "Some of them arrive with a few sweets and clothes for the children and then live off of us [villagers] for the rest of the summer." This is not, however, the preponderant sentiment. When I repeated the above statement to

---

[1] The size of the average family has been considerably reduced over the past generation. This is attributable both to emigration and to a reduction in the number of children born to each family. The lowered birth rate is evidenced by comparative statistics: the average household in the grandparental generation contained 3.8 children; in contemporary Benabarre there is an average of only 1.8 children per family. The difference is due, of course, to a conscious effort to limit family size.

*A part of the housing development being constructed (mainly for summer visitors) on the outskirts of Benabarre.*

others, its spirit was widely denied. One man said, "Nobody looks at costs with the family; everybody's happy enough just getting them all together again."

The principal reason that villagers do not feel exploited by relatives is that most of them have means of redressing the balance. Some village families have recently begun to take brief winter vacations in Barcelona. Those who do' so are families which have relatives there and are able to remain in their city apartments. Or if such a trip is not feasible for the entire family, the children are sent for a few weeks to stay with their aunts and uncles. Villagers who make business trips to the cities and who must remain there for more than a day, also take advantage of the hospitality of relatives. I once questioned two informants about recent trips they had made to Barcelona. Both of them, it turned out, had lodged with relatives. This was becoming a familiar pattern to me and I commented that it was apparently rare for a villager to stay in a hotel. One of them laughingly remarked, "If the hotel owners of Barcelona had to depend on us, they would have gone out of business long ago." He added that there were probably many Benabarrenses who had never lodged in a hotel. But I insisted that it must occassionally occur that villagers find themselves in a strange city in which they have no friends or relatives. My informant answered, "Not necessarily; if they didn't have relatives there they wouldn't have gone to that city in the first place."

Now that many families are attempting to provide their children with secondary education, relatives in the urban setting can aid them in various ways. There are a number of families in Benabarre which have children staying with relatives while they attend schools in Binefar, Huesca, Zaragoza, or Barcelona. This reduces expenses since they avoid the cost of having the children live at the school. Urban relatives can also be of help in finding employment for sons and daughters who leave the village. The desire to establish (*colocar*) children in secure jobs is perhaps the number one preoccupation of village parents. An uncle who is on the Lérida police force can use his influence to secure a position for his nephew as a policeman, in the postoffice, or in some other governmental agency. A cousin employed in a garage in Barcelona may arrange to have his village cousin hired as an apprentice mechanic. A number of villagers are employed in the Barcelona postal service and in an important hydroelectric company because each of these agencies have long-time employees from Benabarre who have used their influence to have other villagers hired.

City people can also provide aid in dealing with the government bureaucracy. By the simple fact of living in the cities they usually have better contacts than villagers, and can place these contacts at the latter's disposal. There are, in addition, less tangible services such as information and advice. When villagers need specialized medical treatment they often act on the recommendation of urban relatives in selecting a clinic or a particular physician. They also follow the lead of relatives on shopping expeditions; whether they seek an automobile or simply new clothing, urbanites can show them the most reasonable places to make their purchases.

On two occasions I even discovered that urbanites were taking a hand in matchmaking between their nieces in Benabarre and young men who work in their companies in Barcelona. The large number of village girls who have married into the cities in recent years is related to the fact that many are spending vacations with urban friends and relatives.

The preceding examples illustrate the reciprocal exchange between relatives. Ties of friendship, however, are nearly as important. The large number of former villagers who live in the cities provides every resident with a great number of potential friends. This is particularly so because of the strong *patria chica* (literally "little country," but meaning homeland) sentiment in the region. Most persons have a remarkably abiding attachment to their native community and region (their *tierra*). I met many individuals who had left Benabarre in their youth, and had lived their entire adult lives in Barcelona, yet they continued to identify as Aragoneses and Benabarrenses. The strength of this sentiment has the practical consequence of forming a bond of solidarity between any two individuals from the village in the metropolitan setting. One of my informants told me that some years ago he was a truck driver for *CAMPSA* (national petroleum monopoly), and was stationed for a few weeks in the Catalonian city of Manresa. He said:

> As soon as I got there I looked up one of the three families from Benabarre I knew were living there. As soon as they saw me they made me stay with them. All the time I was in Manresa they kept me like a son in their home.

These were simply former co-villagers, not relatives. It is, of course, this same *patria chica* phenomenon which induces urbanites to return to Benabarre every year.

## EXTRA-COMMUNITY NETWORKS: POLITICAL IMPLICATIONS

All of the extra-community relationships discussed to this point are formed between persons who conceive of themselves as social equals. Despite the fact that urban relatives often adopt patronizing attitudes toward villagers (see p. 53), there is usually little status difference between them. They all proceed from the same social background and, except in the case of a few urbanites who have been remarkably successful, they are generally on a similar economic plane. Thus the reciprocal ties which unite them are what one anthropologist (Foster 1967:217) has called "colleague contracts" (those which operate between equals) as distinguished from "patron–client contracts" which unite individuals of disparate social status.

By far the largest proportion of ties which villagers maintain outside of the community are of the colleague type. When residents seek aid in dealing with agencies external to the community their first recourse is to turn to sets of relatives and friends. The political implications of this fact should not go unheeded. It is a radical turnabout from the situation a generation ago when most ties that ordinary villagers maintained to the exterior were mediated by community patrons, whom I referred to earlier as "brokers" (pp. 35-36). Today there are virtually no persons in Benabarre who perform such a function. The reason, of course, is that villagers now have multiple channels of contact with the exterior, all of which constitute functional alternatives to dependence on patrons. Therefore most of the services formerly obtained through reliance on a village *padrino*, such as finding employment for children, obtaining protection from arbitrary power, or dealing with governmental agencies, are now managed through sets of interpersonal relationships founded on the relative equality of partners.

The principal tool by which these networks are constructed is what I will refer to as "instrumental friendship" (Wolf 1966). The term refers to the fact that Benabarrenses deliberately enter into relationships—always couched in the idiom of friendship—in which they clearly expect to use the friend, and to be used by him in turn. Friendship serves these purposes because of the strong emphasis (general throughout Spain) placed on loyalty and mutual obligations between friends. As Pitt-Rivers (1954:138) has described the institution in Andalusia:

> To enter into friendship with someone means putting oneself in a state of obligation. This obligation obliges one to meet his request, even though it involves a sacrifice on one's part. One must not, if one can help it, say "no" to a friend. On the other hand accepting a service involves him in an obligation, which he must be ready to repay.

In Benabarre there is an intimate association between the exchange of favors and friendship. If a person accepts a service or token of appreciation from another, he tacitly accepts the proffered *amistad* (friendship). A rejection of these offers, on the other hand, is tantamount to a refusal of friendship. The latter case is illustrated by the behavior of a physician who practiced in Benabarre in 1967-1968. This gentleman made a concerted effort to keep his relations with villagers on a purely professional footing, to avoid, as he expressed it, "becoming entangled in their [villagers'] petty affairs." Consequently, when villagers attempted to present him with gifts (of eggs, fruits, sausages) beyond the payment for his services, both he and his wife adamantly refused to accept them. Villagers soon learned not to make the offers and said about the doctor, "He doesn't want friendship with anybody." The doctor sought to avoid the conflict of interest between the demand that he give special consideration to friends, and his obligation to provide disinterested service to the community as a whole.

An incident which occurred when I had mechanical difficulties with my automobile illustrates a similar conflict. One of my informants (José Pellicer) told me that a good friend of his was a mechanic in the neighboring town of Graus, and that this man could fix my car without any difficulty. We drove to the town but found that the mechanic was tremendously busy with four or five cars waiting for his attention. The mechanic told us that he was too busy and would not be able to attend us that afternoon. I was willing to accept this, but José insisted, saying that we had urgent need of the car. The mechanic replied, "And what about all these people who were here first?" The discussion continued, with the mechanic holding firm, until José played his trump, saying, "That's a fine way to treat a friend from the war," referring to some supposed obligation between them from the distant past. The mechanic was beaten; with a sigh of resignation he picked up his tools and began work on my car.

There is also in the minds of villagers a close association between making the right friends and social mobility. When villagers discuss the qualities of prominent men, or tell a success story, they often say, "He knew how to make all the right friendships," or "He had good friends who helped him." Conversely, it is very common to hear old men in Benabarre who have never been successful bemoan the fact that they were unable to capitalize on their friendships. As one elderly peasant told me:

> Anybody else with the friendships I had would have come out [of the Civil War] on top, but I didn't get anything; that's the way things are. I was a close friend of Llanas, the colonel, and I had lots of other important friendships. But look, I haven't got anything to show for it.

In order to illustrate how these ties operate, particularly in a political sense, I will cite some concrete examples.

The first concerns Medardo Balaguer, one of Benabarre's poultry farmers. Some years ago the village government levied a tax on all families of the community to supplement a grant of state funds for the construction of a new village school. Medardo was dissatisfied with what he considered inequities in the tax allocations made to each family; and since he had no children to attend school anyway, he refused to contribute. Moreover he convinced a number of other families to also withhold their contributions. The mayor and village council were incensed by his actions, and they decided to punish him. Using the pretext of a neighbor's complaint over the noise made by grain milling machinery in his home, they notified him of an obscure ordinance which states that machinery must be placed outside of residential sections of the village unless the owner can meet certain specifications on the reduction of noise.

This was aimed solely at Medardo since the ordinance is almost universally ignored in the community. Benabarre's carpenters, blacksmiths, and butchers all have machinery, most of it noisier than Medardo's, and none were affected. Medardo was in a serious bind because it would be both difficult and inconvenient to move his machinery, and meeting the specifications on noise reduction promised to be expensive. He needed legal advice but there was nowhere to turn in Benabarre. He did not trust Benabarre's only lawyer who was a close friend of the mayor and, Medardo suspected, had probably advised the council in their action against him.

He thereupon made a trip to the provincial capital to visit a friend, Luis Visa, a former villager who now works as a petty functionary in the ministry of justice. Medardo was aware that Luis was not a particularly influential person, but he also knew that in the performance of his duties in the ministry he comes into daily contact with many of the important officials of the province. After Medardo had explained his problem, Luis took him to see a lawyer who works in the ministry and with whom he has *amistad*. The lawyer thought it would be unwise for Medardo to fight the issue and preferable to simply comply with the ordinance requirements for reducing noise. For a nominal fee (because he did this as a favor to his friend Luis) he drew up a plan of how all legal specifications could be met, and lent his prestigious name to the reply to the town hall. Medardo followed his advice to the letter, and after the report was submitted there was no further response from the village government.

The foregoing example illustrates an important principle: namely that any individual's contacts can be greatly expanded by tying into the personal networks of friends and relatives. Thus Medardo was generously aided by a lawyer he had not previously met simply because his friend, Luis, had a close relationship to this gentleman. The *modus operandi* here is what one writer (Boissevain 1966:24-25) has termed the "friend-of-a-friend syndrome": individuals frequently place their personal contacts at the disposal of friends, making possible a considerable extension of the ties available to any individual.

Another illustration of this mechanism is provided by a former mayor of Benabarre who now lives in the provincial capital. He owns a bar–cafe there which is a natural gathering place for villagers when they visit the capital. The owner is not a man of great influence in the city, but he is acquainted with many of the important men of Huesca who frequent his bar. Consequently he is able to aid villagers on occasion by putting them in touch with officials or administrators. An informant explained to me that he once needed some papers approved on a social security matter. The application was submitted to the proper office in Huesca but then weeks passed with no response. The next time he journeyed to the capital he mentioned his difficulty to the bar owner. The latter told him to return to the cafe at half-past two that afternoon when the social security section chief (*jefe*) would come in for his daily cognac. That afternoon the bar owner introduced my informant to the *jefe*, providing him an opportunity to explain his problem. The section chief said he would look into the matter immediately; and, true to his word, the papers were received in the mail three days later. As a former villager and onetime mayor, the bar owner is disposed to mediate ties for almost anyone from Benabarre.

Relationships of this sort have also been utilized by Benabarre's modern farmers and livestock merchants as a means of securing government loans. One such loan was in the gestation stages while I was in Benabarre and I was able to observe the procedure firsthand. Máximo, one of the community's farmer–merchants, learned from the local agricultural extension agent that the government was offering exceptionally favorable terms on loans (of 100,000 *pesetas*, or $1,425) to encourage the planting of apple orchards. The program is designed to introduce fruit crops into the area as part of a campaign to reduce the heavy reliance on cereal cultivation. The loans are interest-free for the first four years and after that, up to ten years, there is a 3 percent interest rate.

Máximo confided to me that he should have no difficulty obtaining the loan since the cousin of his sister-in-law is an official in one of the offices of agrarian affairs in Huesca. He explained that if these applications are to be successful they need a big push (*empujón*) from someone with influence. A few weeks later, accompanied by his brother and sister-in-law, he visited this gentleman who assured them that he would do everything in his power to have the loan approved. But he also imparted the bad news that the loan had to be initiated in Zaragoza rather than through his office. He offered to put in a good word for Máximo there, but admitted that he could not be certain of the outcome.

Máximo was disappointed but remained determined to proceed with the application. I asked him if he would now simply apply and hope that his friend's influence would suffice. He answered no, that he would have to take a more active role. This he did. He drove to Zaragoza and delivered his application personally to the agent in charge. Máximo's intent here was to develop friendly relations with the official. A week later, as had been agreed, the agent came to Benabarre to investigate Máximo's land. However, while the official was in the village he remained very noncommittal, and declined an invitation to lunch in Máximo's home. After he had departed Máximo was not at all convinced that his ultimate decision would be favorable. A few days later, therefore, he made another trip to Zaragoza. He carried in the trunk of his car an entire dry salted ham and went to the agent's home. When the gentlemen appeared at the door, Máximo thanked him for all his trouble of a few days earlier and said that he wanted to give him a small token (*una atención*) of his appreciation. He led him to the car and showed him the ham. Máximo said that the agent's eyes lighted up immediately and he was obviously very pleased. Máximo told me, "As soon as I saw that he was going to accept the ham I knew my loan was as good as approved." And so it eventually was. Máximo summed up his secret of success:

> You see, you've got to be active. Just sitting back won't get you anywhere. You've got to make the right friends and you have to stay on top (*estar encima*) of these matters all the time.

The foregoing examples should give insight into how certain residents order their social universe outside of the community. It would be grossly inaccurate, however, to foster the impression that most villagers have ready access to power and influence, or that there are many who are able to operate as successfully as Máximo in the above example. In Benabarre, as in most societies, a majority of the people are relatively powerless. It is true that all residents have ties outside the village, but it does not follow that all are equally capable of manipulating these relationships to their own advantage. A large number of persons, particularly those referred to earlier as "traditional" farmers and the elderly, have few connections to sources of influence and power outside the community. As one might expect, they are also the individuals most disposed to romanticize the past. Traditional farmers constantly lament the fact that Benabarre no longer contains powerful men who can act as protectors and patrons to them as did the prewar *señoritos*. They complain about disunity and lack of cooperation in the village and attribute it to the fact that there are no important men (*no hay hombres*). Because of the absence of the kind of patronage they seek, it is probably true that many of these villagers experience a greater sense of political impotence today than did their parents a generation ago.

It is exactly the reverse among members of the new middle class. Most of Benabarre's merchants and entrepreneurial farmers have forged close ties to important persons in the provincial bureaucracy and in some of the large commercial firms throughout the region. Such relationships have been instrumental in the loans they have secured for agricultural improvements and for most of the new livestock farms which have been constructed in Benabarre. The example of Máximo demonstrates their capabilities. When he realized that his friend in Huesca might not be able to exert the appropriate influence, he took it upon himself to construct the friendship links demanded by the situation. The ability to forge these network ties to significant individuals and agencies has been a crucial element in their commercial success. As one of Benabarre's grain merchants told me:

> The important thing here is to make friendships with the right people, especially with *ellos* [meaning government people or officials in general]. If you're on their side, the side of the people going up, you're all right. If not, there's nothing for you.

The multiplication of ties between villagers and persons outside of the community has also had important consequences for the local power structure. I alluded to this general point earlier (p. 85) but it merits reiteration. All villagers are in agreement that there are few powerful or influential individuals in contemporary Benabarre. This is especially true, they say, when the leaders of today are compared to the *señoritos* of thirty years ago. The difference is, I think, a genuine one. The former leaders were influential, in part, because they were "brokers," able to manage the contacts between ordinary villagers and the larger society. Today such a degree of control is impossible; the broker function has been fragmented into literally hundreds of sets of private ties between villagers and outsiders. The power which accrued to such intermediaries has therefore vanished. This is certainly a very general tendency in modernizing communities, in Spain as well as other countries. As Stirling (1965:82) has reported for Turkish villages:

> ... the changing economy has great effects on traditional social organisation. ... in general, the main change is the multiplication, for most adult male villagers, of a new private set of more or less impersonal social relations with employers, fellow-workers, officials, and buyers and sellers, different for each individual, all leading out of the village into the national society. A generation ago, such external relations were the prerogative of village leaders. ... This change inevitably opens the structure of village society, and lessens the authority of its leaders.

## INFLUENTIAL HIJOS DEL PUEBLO

Despite the fact that there are few powerful persons in Benabarre, villagers do maintain ties with a class of individuals whom they regard somewhat as patrons. These are the various *hijos* (native sons) of Benabarre who have achieved prominence in the larger society, and who now reside in the towns and cities. They include men from a wide range of occupations: professional people, government officials, clerics, and important business executives. Many of them are descendants of the old bourgeoisie; others are native sons from more humble backgrounds who have met with substantial occupational or economic success. The latter include virtually all of the villagers who have achieved secondary or university education. There are few vocational opportunities for educated persons in Benabarre, and villagers would, at any rate, consider it a waste for an educated son to remain in the community. It is a universal expectation that such persons will emigrate to the cities where it is believed that educational talents can be properly utilized.

These important native sons are associated with the community in much the same manner as the relatives and friends discussed earlier. Their families descend from Benabarre (and some still live in the village) and these *hijos* consider the community their native hearth. Many maintain the family's ancestral home in Benabarre which they use for vacations. They visit every summer, and occasionally in winter when they take advantage of the wild boar hunting in the mountains around Benabarre. Others have built large summer homes on the outskirts of the community. Then some of the families still own farm property in the village and have it cultivated by tractor owners or by the agricultural cooperative.

The main significance of these native sons is that they are of high social status and are generally in much closer touch with spheres of power and influence than is the average resident of Benabarre. For many villagers these *hijos* are the most influential persons with whom they have close personal association. Friendly relations arise quite naturally out of village sociability. When these men and their families vacation in Benabarre they are caught up in a constant round of greetings and social exchange. As mentioned previously, villagers derive a great deal of pleasure from interaction with persons of education and high social status. When, for instance, Benabarrenses explain why summer is such an exciting time they often mention the fact that distinguished visitors are present. "In summer the village comes alive," said one woman. "There are doctors and lawyers and even a marchioness (*marquesa*) who stays with us here." There is also, of course, the desire on the part of villagers to cultivate friendship with these individuals due to the potential utility of the contacts.

It is natural, then, that when Benabarrenses confront a situation which requires the purveyance of influence, they often turn to these prominent individuals. A matter of this kind arose some years ago when the village government backed an ambitious plan to establish a glass factory in Benabarre. Two young Catalonian businessmen discovered that there were relatively rich deposits of silica sand on the outskirts of the village and they conceived the possibility of constructing a factory to produce high quality glass. They were able to convince some of Benabarre's most influential men, as well as a majority of the populace, that it was a feasible project.

Construction was to be financed by selling shares in the factory. About half of the families of the community (and many from surrounding villages) eventually contributed sums of between 1,000 and 2,000 *pesetas* ($16.60—$33.30); and some of the village merchants pooled considerably larger amounts.

In the early stages, however, the plan ran into serious bureaucratic obstacles. The backers of the project were unable to obtain the necessary legal permission to establish a factory of the kind they envisioned in Benabarre. The village *secretario* made various trips to official centers in the provincial capital but to no avail. He was told that there were specific regulations against building such a factory in a community of Benabarre's size, and that the project could only be approved on the highest levels of government. Finally, the *secretario* headed a delegation of villagers which journeyed to Madrid to petition for a hearing in the Ministry of Commerce. Upon arrival, however, they were blocked at the front desks of the ministry and failed completely to secure an appointment with officials.

With failure of the entire project staring them in the face, the *secretario* decided, as a last resort, to telephone one of the *hijos* of Benabarre who lives in Madrid, Don Joaquín Arsac. This gentleman is an important official in the government petroleum monopoly; his family is descended from Benabarre and he visits the community every summer (and has recently built a large summer home overlooking the community). When the *secretario* called him and explained their problem, Don Joaquín very graciously offered his services. He made a telephone call to one of his personal friends in the ministry and asked him to aid the villagers in any way he could. The delegation was granted an interview the same afternoon. The ministry official dictated some minor revisions in the proposal and then had it stamped with official approval. The delegation was then able to return in triumph to Benabarre.

This same native son has exerted influence on villagers' behalf on a number of occasions. It is difficult to determine exactly what return he receives for his favors. When I questioned villagers whom he had benefitted they usually responded that he was a very generous person (*muy noble*) who did these things out of love for his native village. It is clear, however, that Don Joaquín is treated very respectfully by most residents. When he visited Benabarre in the spring of 1968, Benabarre's innkeeper told me that we would have to suspend our interview sessions for a week because he would be busy taking care of the official's needs. And when his summer home was built in the community, members of the village government went to great lengths to accommodate his various requests. Don Joaquín is also given considerate treatment in the village shops and is the recipient of occasional gifts of food and other small services from villagers. The problem, however, is that meaningful reciprocity with a person who is so remote from village affairs is very difficult; there is very little he could want from villagers in return. It may be simply as I was told by one of Don Joaquín's relatives that, "The man thrives on praise."

Another of the influential *hijos* of Benabarre (also a descendant of a notable family) is now a high ranking military officer in Zaragoza. When a boy from Benabarre is drafted, or there is concern over a matter involving the military, this man is frequently appealed to. The following account is one among many involving this individual. In 1959 the nephew of one of my informants was drafted. The boy came to his uncle (my informant) to ask if he would write him a letter of introduction which he could deliver to Don Sebastian (the officer) in Zaragoza. His uncle agreed. He had been part of this family's clientele prior to the Civil War, and considers that even today there is a great deal of *amistad* between them. The boy carried the letter to the officer's home soon after reporting for duty in Zaragoza. When the officer had read the letter he insisted that the boy stay with them for dinner. During the meal Don Sebastian asked if there was anything that he could do. The boy replied that he had recently become a shoemaker in Benabarre and he wondered if it would be possible for him to practice his trade while in the army. Don Sebastian said that it could be easily arranged. As a result the boy spent most of his tour of duty as a shoemaker for officers in Zaragoza.

A further example is that of a lawyer in Barcelona who is from one of Benabarre's farm households. He has risen to a position of influence in a government-controlled hydroelectric company. He is known to have helped many villagers in the urban setting and has been instrumental in the hiring of various village youths as drivers and technicians. By far the most elaborate and best attended funeral I witnessed while I was in Benabarre was held at the death of this lawyer's mother-in-law. The woman died in Barcelona but was buried in a hamlet close to Benabarre. When I registered surprise at the considerable show of mourning for a woman who had not lived in Benabarre for years, my informants answered that it was to pay respect to the lawyer: "People here owe him lots of favors."

My fieldnotes contain a large number of similar instances in which villagers have asked help from prominent native sons. The cases recorded above, however, are sufficient to suggest the character of these relationships. The ties bear close resemblance to the network linkages to urban friends and relatives discussed earlier. The difference resides in the fact that, whereas the former operate between persons who consider themselves social equals, the links to influential native sons involve a significant difference in status. As such the latter can be considered a species of patron–client relationship. Yet I am hesitant to employ the term because the dependency suggested by the word "clientage" is virtually nonexistent. Villagers do not consider the occasional resort to an urban native son as being of the same class with the relations maintained to Benabarre's prewar elite, in which there was an ongoing dependency and subordination to the patron. In former times indebtedness to village *padrinos* often had to be repaid in demeaning political or personal service. Since the present-day benefactors do not reside in Benabarre, they can hardly expect this kind of support in return for favors granted. None of them is involved in village government and none takes part in the factional struggles which occasionally ripple the surface of the community. Consequently the relationships have little discernible impact on the local power structure.

## INSTITUTIONS AND NETWORKS

In the preceding sections I have dealt with the relationship between the village and the larger society from the perspective of the individual. I have described the major means by which individuals (or families) in Benabarre are linked to other persons in the larger society. In so doing I have concentrated on concrete systems of social relations. There is, of course, an entirely different manner in which the relationship could be analyzed, namely, in terms of the institutional framework. One could show how particular institutions, such as village government, the parish church, the Civil Guard outpost and so forth, are connected to an ascending series of parent institutions in the wider society. The result would be a description of the administrative and ecclesiastical hierarchies through which the community is bound to entities in the nation as a whole.

I have quite deliberately emphasized the social relations perspective at the expense of the latter. My justification for so doing is that I believe that these networks of social relations are of critical importance in understanding contemporary Spanish society. This is partly the case due to the state of transition in which Spain presently finds herself; it is also attributable to certain unique characteristics of Spanish development. Elucidation of these statements requires that we look briefly at the larger context of Spain's modernization.

As emphasized earlier, Spain is undergoing a rapid change from what was a fundamentally agrarian society to an incipiently industrialized state. Much of this development has occurred within the time span of one generation. The most pervasive transformation has occurred in the economic and technological sphere, while aspects of the social and political order have been less radically affected. This is as one might expect. Anthropologists have often shown that even in instances of radical historical change, societies are rarely transformed completely. Customs and institutions which were integral parts of the previous society are carried over, occasionally with only slight modification, into the present. This is partly attributable to the fact that people continue to behave in terms of norms and standards which were assimilated at an early point in life and it takes time for such standards to change.

It would therefore be unreasonable to suppose that Spanish society should rid itself, in the brief span of one generation, of many characteristics of its preindustrial past. A more likely expectation would be that many of the organizational mechanisms of the earlier society will continue to be relied upon despite the emergence of new institutions within the context of industrial society. One anthropologist (Leeds 1965:380) has attempted to summarize what he considers are the basic organizational principles of preindustrial as compared to industrial societies. In the preindustrial situation,

> With the given technology, agrarian and communicational, the social order is necessarily markedly structured around localities and localized communities. Therefore, face-to-face, kin, pseudokin, and other personal ties, often highly ritualized, appear as major organizational mechanisms of the total society.

Industrial societies, on the other hand, are largely organized in terms of formal, supra-local institutions. Leeds continues (1965:380-81):

> The fundamental ecological pattern of industrial states is multiregional, tending toward global, and consequently, the societies tend to be exocentric, politically and economically; to maximize translocal relationships at the expense of locality

and community relationships; and to operate through highly organized supralocal institutions and associations.

In developing countries, those which are at some point in the transition from the first type of social system to the second, we should expect to find both types of organizational mechanisms in complex association (Leeds 1965:383, 401). This is, in fact, one of the most remarkable features of contemporary Spanish society. Virtually all institutions are paralleled, or significantly supplemented, by sets of highly personal relationships. Thus the mere existence of formal institutions does not necessarily imply that they operate on objective principles. The belief, for instance, that the personal factor significantly enters into the operation of Spanish officialdom is universal in Benabarre, and indeed, among Spaniards generally. An opinion survey among Spanish youth, conducted in 1966, reveals the general state of opinion. Adolescents in various sections of the country were asked the question of how they believe most official matters are accomplished in Spain. A large majority answered either by "using friends" or "seeking a good recommendation"; only very few (approximately 9 percent) said by "following the normal channels." The author of the opinion survey summarizes the attitudes of his respondents toward Spanish officialdom (Buceta-Facorro 1966:189):

> All of this confirms just how strong is the belief among our young people that our institutions do not function in the manner of a formal structure based on objective rules and on the equality of all citizens, but rather that it is necessary to make use of an informal structure based on relations of friendship or interest which substitutes objectivity, the basis of a legal State, for the subjectivity of personal relations; . . . the immorality which the young people condemn, in reference to our institutions, is the immorality of arbitrariness, the immorality of operating on subjective and particularistic principles instead of on objective principles.

A second explanation for the importance of personal networks in Benabarre (and in rural Spain generally) has to do with certain characteristics of the Spanish political system. The authoritarian and highly centralized Spanish polity has placed limitations on the development of institutions which could serve to mediate relations between local communities and higher levels of authority. The kinds of intermediate institutions which represent the interest of peasants and workers in many other countries are either absent or are weakly developed in Spain. Mass political parties are nonexistent; labor unions exist more on paper than in fact; and there is nothing which could be considered vigorous local government.

In theory there is a single political party in Benabarre, the *Falange* or Spanish Fascist party. Yet only the locally appointed officials play any role in party concerns, and even they are indifferent participants. The party has no locally committed body of supporters (though it did in the 1940s and early 1950s), it never operates as a unit, and for all intents and purposes exists only in name. Benabarre's labor and agrarian organizations are only slightly more effective. All unions in Spain are part of the government controlled "vertical syndicates" structure. The unions were created and imposed by the government rather than having been formed by free association of laborers. Therefore, most peasants and workers are members of a syndicate whether they choose to be or not. All of Benabarre's farmers are theoretically members of the *Hermandad* (brotherhood) of farmers and stockbreeders. The average peasant, however, tends to regard the *Hermandad* as more a mechanism of government control than as an agency committed to his interests, and most are profoundly apathetic toward union activities. Only two meetings of the *Hermandad* were called during the fourteen months I was in Benabarre and less than twenty persons attended each meeting. The organization plays such an insignificant role in the lives of most farmers that, when directly asked, many cannot say what the *Hermandad* is or what it is supposed to do.

Given the absence or weak development of these mediating institutions, it is understandable that villagers seek other means of representing their interests, through friends, relatives, and personal contacts.

## THE CHARACTER OF VILLAGE GOVERNMENT

The most significant institutional means by which the community is related to the larger society is through village government. Benabarre represents the terminus of a hierarchy of political and administrative power which originates in Madrid and extends down through the provincial capital.

Municipal administration in Spain is part of a highly centralized system of government which provides little scope for community autonomy or local initiative. The mayor is appointed for an indefinite term of office by the provincial governor and he may be removed from office by an act of the Ministry of the Interior. One of the mayor's titles is "Delegate of the Government" which expresses his dependence on higher authority. The second important official of village government is the *secretario* or town clerk. He is responsible for interpreting laws and regulations for the mayor and council, and is the caretaker of day-to-day administration. Since his position is also appointive, villagers have virtually no voice in the selection of officials who have the greatest influence over village government.

The mayor is, in theory, in full control of government. He presides over the council and bears responsibility (along with the Civil Guard) for maintaining public order and for ensuring that all government laws and regulations are obeyed in the community. In practice, however, the situation may be very different. In Benabarre and in every community I was able to observe, the *secretario* was the most influential official. In 1967-1968 Benabarre's *secretario* made most of the crucial governmental decisions and he was the most frequent initiator of community action.

There is a rather simple explanation for this deviation between theory and practice. The *secretario* is the only salaried official in the government and he usually also has education and professional preparation. As a paid official he is able to devote undivided attention to his duties. He gains familiarity with all aspects of administration and his expertise in these matters is usually sufficient to give him de facto control of the town hall. The mayor, on the other hand, serves without remuneration. Since he must devote his major energies to earning a living, the mayorship can be no more than a part-time activity. Furthermore, he is unlikely to have extensive education. Mayors typically do not understand the complexities of administration and they have neither the time nor inclination to learn.

In some of the small villages in the immediate vicinity of Benabarre the domination by *secretarios* is very pronounced. The clerk in a neighboring community is often referred to as the village dictator. He is aware of this appellation and not at all disturbed by it. He once told me, "If anything at all is to be done in these villages the *secretario* has to be a dictator." Another town clerk who resides in a village to the north of Benabarre handles the administration for his village as well as for fifteen small hamlets in the hinterland. I once accompanied him as he visited four of the town halls on his circuit. In each village he sent a child to fetch the mayor in order to obtain his signature on miscellaneous documents and reports. As we were waiting in the town hall for one of the mayors the *secretario* explained:

> In these villages the *secretarios* are the real leaders; they have to do everything. If the mayor can read and sign his name that's all that's necessary. The man who is mayor of this village is a farmer and it's always a problem for me to get him away from his fields long enough to sign his name.

When the mayor did arrive the *secretario* placed some papers before him, briefly stated what they were for, and asked him to sign. The mayor started to write but on the wrong line. The *secretario* said, impatiently, "No, not there, here," indicating the proper space with an insistent tap of his finger. The mayor apologized and signed where he should.

In Benabarre the *secretario* was not quite the dominant figure as are these secretarios of the smaller villages. Yet the difference is one of degree. A number of community betterment projects were implemented during the period I spent in Benabarre and the *secretario* was the motive force behind each one. When the community swimming pool was built the project was beset by various delays and interruptions, and it often appeared to villagers that the pool would never be successfully completed. As I investigated the matter I quickly discovered that the *secretario* was the only source of reliable information concerning the status of construction. Other villagers, including members of the town council, were uninformed about even major aspects of the project. It was the *secretario* who negotiated personally with the contracting companies, managed the financial affairs, and single-handedly supervised nearly every detail.

All of the above examples illustrate a characteristic feature of village government: few persons are involved in the decision-making process at any level. Even in regard to matters of crucial significance to the community, responsibility remains in the hands of officials. If they do not attend to such matters, nobody else will. In the summers of 1967 and 1968, for example, it became evident that Benabarre's water supply was inadequate to the demands being placed on it by the increased summer population and the various new livestock farms. On certain days in July and August many village homes were left entirely without running water. The problem did not lie in the adequacy of the water supply, but rather in the limited capacity of the pipe system which conducts water to the village. Nearly everybody was aware of the problem, yet when the shortage caused serious inconvenience there was no discernible effort to do anything about it. In response to my questions, informants stated that they hoped something would be done, and that the *secretario* should petition the state for funds to build a new conduit system. The characteristic attitude, however, was that it was the government's problem rather than a community problem, and that the only means of remedying the situation was through a grant of funds from the state. If such funds were not forthcoming, villagers were prepared to accept considerable inconvenience.

Benabarrenses do not conceive of local government as an agency they control and they rarely think of it as an extension of the community. The most common attitude, in fact, is one of protest against it as an agency which conveys objectional demands to them from higher authority.

# 6 / Conclusions: balance sheet on modernization

In this final chapter I want to make some general observations on what Benabarrenses have gained, and what they may have lost, in modernization. In the main these observations derive from the way villagers themselves perceive the changes occurring, or which have occurred, in the community. At the end of the chapter I will have a few remarks which more nearly reflect my own thinking.

## LOSS OF COMMUNITY

Certainly one of the most negative consequences of modernization, in the minds of villagers, is that they believe it has brought the decline of their community. There is widespread agreement that Benabarre used to be a more important village than it is today. There are various sources of this belief, but the most significant stems from the preoccupation over emigration and the departure of young people. Many villagers have been demoralized by the population loss Benabarre has experienced, and this has given rise to considerable concern over the ultimate fate of the community. There was even a period in the 1950s when many individuals wondered if the village would survive. The economy was at a low ebb and it appeared that a large number of residents were leaving, or planning to leave, for the cities.

Then in the 1960s the growth of the livestock industry and the tourist trade substantially bolstered the local economy. The consequent prosperity did a great deal to dispel the fear that Benabarre would follow the same road to extinction traversed by many of the smaller villages in the mountain hinterland. Nevertheless, the fact that a large proportion of the young people choose to desert the area seems to confirm for residents the relative insignificance of their community. And of course the feeling is reinforced in most contacts with urbanites.

Another cause of concern is that population loss has been accompanied by a marked attenuation of local social life and community culture. Villagers frequently remark that, "There's no longer any life in this village" (*Ya no hay vida en este pueblo*), or that the community has a poor social atmosphere. Adult informants asserted that there were a great many recreational events in Benabarre when they were young, but that almost all of them have now disappeared. Persons over forty recall that Benabarre had a village orchestra, a *fútbol* (soccer) team, street dances on Saturday nights and on holidays, occasional amateur theatrical performances (*comedias*), and traditional dances and pageantry accompanied the major festivals. Certain of these activities continued for a period after the Civil War but, except for dances held in summer and certain folkloric events during the patron saint festival, none exists today.

The demise of recreational activities is frequently attributed to the fact that there are so few young persons in the community. Villagers say that such activities depend upon the support of adolescents and post-adolescents, and with so many from this age group living away (as students or they have emigrated), the events have expired for lack of support. It is difficult to evaluate this assertion. In 1967-1968 there were between sixty and seventy youths in the age category from fourteen to twenty-four who lived in the community for most of the year. While this is a small number in relation to the total population, it does seem that it was sufficient to support more activities than took place.

The adolescents who remain in Benabarre frequently complain that they are bored. Almost everyone agrees that something should be done to create a better social atmosphere, but little has been accomplished. Some years prior to my fieldwork the village priest attempted to organize a youth group to provide recreational activities for teen-agers. There was some initial enthusiasm for the project, but then attendance fell off at the weekly meetings and the priest abandoned the effort. He now says that this illustrates a significant defect of villagers; "They start out on things and then fail to carry them through." The adolescents, however, have a different explanation. They say the youth group failed because the priest would not allow dancing, of which he disapproves; and since dancing is their premier interest, they saw no point in continuing.

An additional reason for the decline of recreational activities has to do with the character of village youth. Benabarre's adolescents are the most urban-oriented group in the community. They are the first generation to have been heavily exposed to mass communications (especially radio and television), and the impact has been considerable. They share in a general "youth culture" which transcends localities everywhere in Spain. They read many of the same popular magazines, worship the pop singers, and dance to the same rock tunes as their counterparts in Barcelona.

The degree to which Benabarre's young people respond to urban derived fads and styles was one of the genuine revelations of my fieldwork. The considerable geographical separation between Benabarre and major cities had led me to expect a certain degree of cultural isolation as well. But as far as the young people were concerned, this was negligible. In 1967, for example, the miniskirt (*minifalda*) made its first widespread appearance in Spain. There was a time lag of only a matter of weeks between the appearance of this style on the streets of Madrid and Barcelona and its appropriation by girls in Benabarre. Furthermore, village girls seemed determined to wear their skirts as short as women in the cities. Also in 1967 the first teen-age males identifiable as "hippies" were observed (with any frequency) on the streets of Barcelona. Almost simultaneously one of the village youths allowed his hair to grow, cultivated a moustache and sideburns, and began wearing a medallion around his neck.

This quest for urban sophistication is associated with a lack of interest in village traditions, which appear to many teen-agers as trivial. This attitude was illustrated

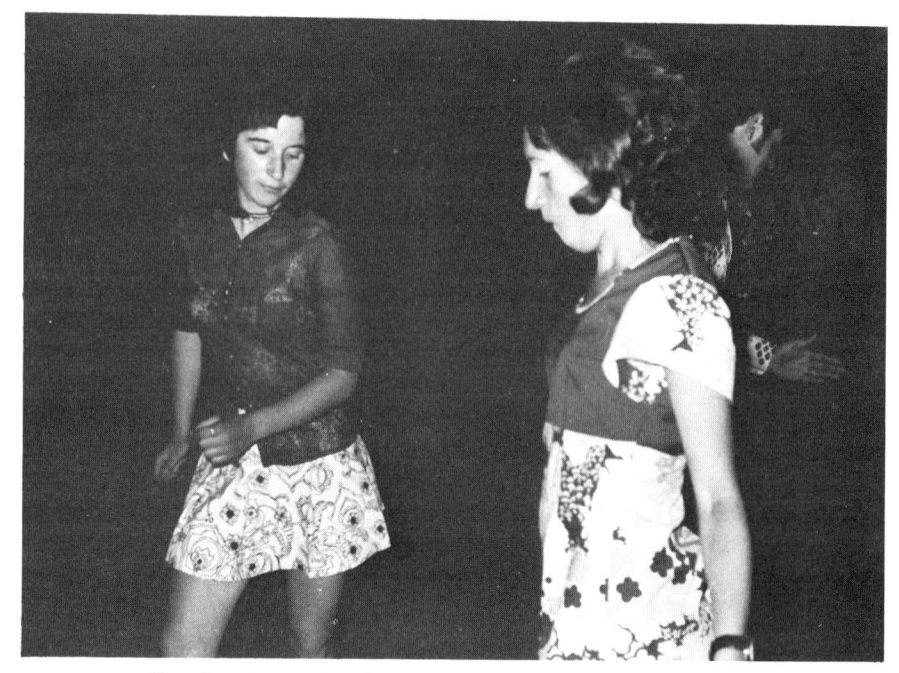

*Benabarre's youth culture: two girls gyrate to rock music.*

on the occasion of Benabarre's patron saint festivals which I observed in 1967 and 1968.

The festival is in honor of Saint Medardo and is held in early June. There were formerly a large number of community or "folk" events associated with the celebration. In the early years of this century a tree was brought in from the forest and erected in the central plaza. Various plays and skits were enacted which, according to the description of my elderly informants, involved a great deal of slapstick and earthy humor. These events have all been lost (most of them early in the century) except for the *pastoradas*—a dialogue between two shepherds who recite a humorous story in rhyme. Even the *pastoradas* suffered a period of eclipse prior to the Civil War, but then were resurrected afterwards through the efforts of a Falangist mayor. However in 1967 the *pastoradas* failed to arouse much enthusiasm. Approximately 200 persons were on hand as spectators; but about half of them were urban visitors or people from the surrounding hamlets of Aler, Sagarras Bajas, and Caladrones. Many of my informants (all of whom had strongly urged me to attend) were absent. When I later questioned them about this a typical reply was, "If you've seen it once that's enough; it's the same every year." The persons most apathetic towards it were the teen-agers and young adults. The twenty-year-old daughter of one of my informants expressed the feeling of most of her peers when she said about the *pastoradas*, "Personally I can't stand them." In 1968 the event was cancelled altogether. The cancellation was a disappointment to some of the old folks. When I told an old man in a neighboring hamlet that they would not be performed he firmly declared that he would not attend the festival. Benabarre's teen-agers were, as far as I could tell, totally unconcerned.

The patron saint procession was also cancelled in the *fiestas* of 1967. The purpose of the procession is to carry the image of Saint Medardo to a shrine in the hills above the village. The image is accompanied by costumed dancers who beat out a rhythmic cadence with special sticks (*palitrocs*). The procession was officially announced in the festival calendar, but at the scheduled hour of departure only the priest, dancers, and a handful of participants had appeared. The priest delayed the procession for forty minutes, but when no more participants arrived he cancelled it altogether. The *secretario*, who was aware that I was waiting to take photographs, came to apologize, saying, "Now you see what's happening; all the typical events (*cosas típicas*) in these villages are disappearing."

The preceding account should not imply that the festival as a whole is in decline. Apathy is only displayed toward "traditional" events, or elements of community culture such as processions, skits, and folklore. On the other hand, all *fiesta* elements which are a part of contemporary urban culture are popular and gain active support. During the 1967 *fiestas* a mobile carnival troupe set up game and contest booths in the central plaza. There was balloon popping with darts, a cork rifle shoot, various games of chance and rides for the children. All of the booths had continual crowds. Then in contrast to the scant support given the *pastoradas* and procession, there was a large turnout for the nightly dances. A small dance band was hired from a neighboring town which beat out strident rock music for three consecutive nights. A majority of villagers, their guests, and hundreds of others from surrounding communities appeared in the plaza to dance, drink, or simply to observe the festivities.

The above description demonstrates the tendency for elements of local culture to become submerged in the preference for urban-derived models of behavior. The tendency can, however, be observed in other than just ritual. A similar preference is exemplified in house construction. Most of the houses in Benabarre are very ancient and, from the standpoint of urban visitors and foreigners, are also very beautiful. However Benabarrenses have little appreciation for old things and they readily tear down the centuries-old facades of their homes to replace them with flat, stuccoed exteriors (which are imitations of the apartments being built in the cities). Urban intellectuals who visit the village often complain that great architectural and artistic treasures are being destroyed. Villagers merely shrug off these comments. The new houses are more comfortable and convenient, and the new facade announces to all that a "modern" family resides within. The same appreciation of newness is seen in house interiors. Villagers often remove rustic walnut tables and chairs to replace them with rickety formica furniture. When they renovate the dining rooms they usually plaster over the exposed pine ceiling beams, a feature of Aragonese houses which seem to captivate everyone but the natives.

The complaint (mentioned above) that there is very little "life" (*vida*) in the community also refers to the fact that there has been a marked reduction in the intensity of social relations. Whenever I discussed the past with villagers they made it clear that the village was formerly a more solid community. They say there was greater unity, people were engrossed in the same local concerns, and gossip and local politics were of more absorbing interest. This was not an opinion of just a few persons; all the adult and elderly people voiced more or less the same judgment. One woman expressed it as follows:

> People stay in their houses now and are only concerned with their own families. They aren't involved with others like they used to be. The women here used to visit and sew together and go into the houses. Nobody does that anymore.

What this woman and others remark is an unmistakable trend toward "atomization" of community social life. Neighborhood gatherings and informal clusters of friends have become less significant than they were only a few years earlier. Villagers say that there used to be sewing circles of women in most *barrios* of Benabarre. A group of women and their daughters would sit together and sew in the street before the doorway of one of the houses. Men had similar groupings. The men of each neighborhood would gather on warm evenings to relax and converse. People were more willing to enter the homes of their neighbors, and there was more general visiting.

The waning importance of such groupings and the lessened intensity of social relations seems to be correlated with the "opening up" of the village to the outside. As villagers have become progressively involved in extra-community social relations the village has declined as a focus of interest and attention. This became particularly evident to me when I sought informants for the village census. Two individuals who are members of the "new middle class" offered to help me but I was surprised to discover that they knew relatively little even about some of the families in their section of the village. They gave inaccurate information regarding how many children certain families had, they did not know whether the children were studying or working in the towns, and so forth. One of them, when he realized he could not provide some of the information, told me that I would have to utilize some of the old people. "They pay attention to everything that goes on in the village and to other families," he said. "I'm too involved in my own affairs to pay attention to those things." I did find the old people to be more reliable sources for this kind of information.

The difference seems to be explained by the fact that, for the elderly, Benabarre is the only status arena which has ever been of significance to them. Their prestige and social standing has always been bound up in the relatively closed social universe of the village. They have been, and continue to be, concerned with all that occurs in the community. The village entrepreneurs, on the other hand, operate within much wider orbits. Their status and position is validated in contacts with business associates, urbanites, and the influential men of neighboring communities. Benabarre no longer contains their aspirations and it composes only one segment of their relevant social universe.

There is also the very concrete matter of diffusion of interests. It must be kept in mind that a majority of village families have been divided by emigration, and the importance of these external ties was demonstrated in the preceding chapter. Families which have children working or studying in the cities have concerns which continually direct their attention outward. It seems reasonable, therefore, to suggest that the internal organization of a community in which a majority of villagers' primary social ties are contained within the village, becomes very different from the organization of one in which strategic social ties expand beyond the community. The difference is manifested in a decline in the intensity of social life.

## THE ECONOMIC AND POLITICAL DIMENSION

While the impact of modernization on the community's social and cultural life is evaluated negatively by most villagers, attitudes shift markedly when the matter is viewed from the perspective of economic or political change.

All villagers recognize that there has been considerable rise in standard of living in Benabarre in the past two decades. As emphasized earlier, economic improvement is not evenly distributed; certain villagers have been more favorably affected than others. Nevertheless, virtually everyone agrees that he is better off today than he (or his family) was twenty years ago. "There was a great deal of poverty (*mucha miseria*) in those days," is a very common preface to discussions about the past. One of my informants, a woman of sixty years, says she cannot tolerate persons of her generation who romanticize the past. She told me:

> When the old men start talking about the old days I cut them off quick. I say to them, 'I'm sorry I even knew those times; they were bad and are better forgotten!'

She cited an example of the kind of poverty she experienced in her youth:

> I remember one day I told my mother that I liked salad, that it would be nice if we could have it more often. But my mother told me, 'No daughter, I can't make salad because I would have to use a lot of oil.' So you can see how wretched we were ... we couldn't even eat foods which now everyone thinks are necessary.

This informant was more vehement in her denunciation of the old days than many others, but she was no exception. When elderly villagers are asked about the past they readily launch into descriptions of the former poverty; and some even refer to the present (beginning around 1960), in contrast, as the period of "*la abundancia*" (affluence, abundance). They say that now everybody has enough to eat, all can dress adequately, and they are able to provide a decent life for their children.

This is not to say that there are no people who are recognized as poor. There are approximately thirty households in Benabarre which get along on very little money income. Most of these are "incomplete" families: elderly widows and widowers who can do very little work, and peasant couples who are childless, or whose children have emigrated. Many of these households in 1968 had annual money incomes of less than 35,000 *pesetas* (about $500). But even these families are not destitute. Benabarre's priest considers that there are no families sufficiently impoverished to qualify for church sponsored charity (*caritas*). However, he does occasionally distribute *caritas* food gifts to eight individuals or families who are thought to be the real *desgraciados* (unfortunates) of the community.

When these poor families are compared to wealthy members of the new middle class (see p. 70) it is evident that there is considerable economic disparity in Benabarre. Nevertheless, economic leverage has not been translated into social or political subservience. Benabarre's entrepreneurs have not become patrons to other members of the community. They are, for the most part, a hardheaded economic class. If they employ others they do so on a rational, cost-accounting basis, and they de-emphasize personal obligations toward their workers.

The poor, on the other hand, do not expect, nor would they appreciate, paternalistic treatment from the newly prosperous members of the community. Mere wealth has not been sufficient to place the new middle class significantly above others in a social sense. Villagers are intimately familiar with the backgrounds of all these men, and family origins and education are influential criteria in placing individuals within the status hierarchy. I repeatedly heard comments about Benabarre's new entrepreneurs, or about their wives, to the effect that they were no better than anybody else. "Matías is no better than I am; he only went to school for four years like the rest of us"; or "Pilar puts on airs now but what can that mean to us when we know she was out guarding sheep when she was a girl?" There is, quite simply, a reluctance to concede superiority to persons of the same general social background. It is conceivable that in the future economic differences may form the basis of a more rigid class structure. I do not expect this to occur, however, as long as the cities and the industrial sector continue to absorb the excess rural population.

Therefore one of the clearest effects of modernization in Benabarre has been to remove the conditions which sustained hierarchy in ordinary social relations. The subservience—even lackeyism—which villagers remember in their dealings with the former elite are almost totally absent today. Many of my informants mentioned this as one of the most beneficial changes to have occurred. They recall the manipulation of the common people by venal lawyers and landowners in the past. Such a situation could not exist today, they say, because villagers are more independent and they are wiser.

It is worth mentioning, however, that the new egalitarianism does not receive unstinted praise. There are a large number of persons in Benabarre who attribute the decline of the village to the fact that so many important families have emigrated. Persons of this opinion (mostly the elderly) say that Benabarre lacks individuals of sufficient stature and "pull" (*mano*) to secure benefits for the village from the government. Some years ago, as a measure of political centralization, the government transferred the regional court from Benabarre to the city of Barbastro. A number of my informants claimed that this could never have occurred over the opposition of the influential families of the prewar period. Others told me that if the *señoritos* still resided in Benabarre the village would not be losing population. "They would have brought industry here," said one informant. "They had influence in all the ministries in Madrid." It appears that many of these individuals are more mindful of the benefits to be gained through patronage than they are of some of the political disabilities which accompanied such a system.

## FINAL REMARKS

As the preceding account suggests, it is difficult for an observer to remain unmoved by the spectacle of transformation occurring in rural Spain. As I studied the process I often had mixed emotions. As an anthropologist part of my mission was to study the society and culture of Spanish peasantry. Yet what I found in Benabarre was that peasants, along with their entire way of life, were virtually disappearing. Households which have been in existence for a century or more were being abandoned; healthy men could not marry simply because they were peasants; a whole class of small farmers apparently have very little future; and age-old customs were being discarded and forgotten. One naturally feels sympathy for the multiple casualties produced in the rural revolution.

On the other hand, to adopt a tragic stance would be senseless. The dissolution of many aspects of rural Spain will certainly be lamented by no one. Large sections of the Spanish countryside have been centers of poverty and distress for centuries. Population pressure on inadequate resources, combined with very inequitable distribution of land, have permitted the average peasant or agricultural laborer only a small margin above the subsistence needs of himself and his family. Since the time of Charles III in the eighteenth century, land reform and other attempts to improve the lot of the peasant have been recurrent themes of Spanish political life. None of the various schemes for land redistribution have been effectively applied; but even if they had it is hard to imagine that they would have yielded a permanent solution to Spain's agrarian problem. As long as the unfavorable balance between population and cultivable land obtained, redistribution could have provided no more than temporary relief.

Emigration to the cities has provided a genuine answer to the problem. One author (Herr 1971:254) has recently summarized the salutary effects of the rural exodus:

> Thus began, without advance planning what one Spaniard has called 'the most singular agrarian reform of all time.' Emigration was the most effective, indeed the indispensable, way to raise the standard of living of rural Spaniards. So long as masses of peasants weighed down the rural economy, forcing the use of inefficient, outdated forms of production to keep them all busy, they were condemned to poverty. . . . Only large scale emigration could reduce the absolute number of agricultural workers and make possible a solution to the centuries old agrarian problem.

The rise in standard of living in Benabarre and throughout the rest of rural Spain would have been impossible if population had continued to increase on the land.

Too often these beneficial effects of emigration go unnoticed. There is a large body of opinion in Spain which views the rural exodus as the manifestation of a diseased countryside. These commentators suggest that Spanish peasants are being driven out of their villages by intolerable conditions, and they often urge the government to initiate programs to "rescue" Spanish agriculture. Such a viewpoint is not limited to Spaniards. In a recent article on Andalusia by an American anthropologist (Mintz 1972:54) emigration is referred to as the "sickness of depopulation" without a suggestion that long-term benefits may also accrue. My response to this point of view is to encourage students of rural Spain to ask villagers if they are better off today than they were twenty years ago. I have put this question to scores of peasants in Aragon, Catalonia and Castile; the answer, with rare exceptions, is that they are incomparably better off.

There are other, equally significant consequences of the rural transformation. One of the great problems of Spanish history has revolved about the division between the small upper classes who have managed the country's political system, and the large masses of common folk in the countryside who have had very little to do with national affairs. Poverty, illiteracy, and isolation effectively barred them from playing any more positive role. The attempts in Spain for more than a century and a half to establish representative political institutions have always foundered on the obstacles presented by a backward and indifferent electorate (Carr 1966: 369-70). *Caciques* and self-serving politicians have invariably been able to manipulate their followers and manage opinion in the villages and towns. And as Richard Herr has pointed out (1971:262-83), the Spanish peasantry has often been an active ally of forces on the national level which have sustained hierarchical and authoritarian institutions.

The change which is occurring in the countryside is therefore bound to affect the Spanish political equation. The integration of villagers into the orbit of urban culture has enabled them to participate in national life as never before. Moreover, the education they are providing their children will equip the latter with skills and opportunities unavailable to their parents. And whether the peasant is transformed by becoming an entrepreneurial farmer, or by becoming a factory worker, in either case he will be more capable of recognizing and defending his political interests than any previous generation.

# References cited

Aceves, Joseph, 1971, *Social Change in a Spanish Village*. Cambridge, Mass.: Schenkman Publishing Co.
Anderson, Charles W., 1970, *The Political Economy of Modern Spain: Policy-Making in an Authoritarian System*. Madison, Wisconsin: University of Wisconsin Press.
Anlló-Vázquez, Juan, 1966, *Estructura y Problemas del Campo Español*. Madrid: Editorial Cuadernos para el Diálogo.
*Anuario Estadístico de España, Año 1968*. Madrid: Instituto Nacional de Estadística.
*Anuario Estadístico de España, Año 1971* (Edición Manual). Madrid: Instituto Nacional de Estadística.
Bailey, F. G., 1971, "The Peasant View of the Bad Life," in *Peasants and Peasant Societies*, ed. by Teodor Shanin. Middlesex, England: Penguin Books (article first published in 1966).
Barrett, Richard A., 1972, "Social Hierarchy and Intimacy in a Spanish Town," *Ethnology*, Vol. XI, No. 4, 386-398.
Beardsley, Richard K., et. al., 1959, *Village Japan*. Chicago: University of Chicago Press.
Black, C. E., 1966, *The Dynamics of Modernization*. New York: Harper & Row (Harper Torchbooks edition).
Bohannan, Paul, 1963, *Social Anthropology*. New York: Holt, Rinehart and Winston.
Boissevain, Jeremy, 1966, "Patronage in Sicily," *Man*, Vol. 1, No. 1.
Buceta-Facorro, Luis, 1966, *La Juventud ante los Problemas Sociales*. Madrid: Editorial Doncel.
Carr, Raymond, 1966, *Spain: 1808-1939*. Oxford: Oxford University Press.
Foster, George M., 1967, *Tzintzuntzan: Mexican Peasants in a Changing World*. Boston: Little, Brown.
Halpern, Joel M., 1965, "The Rural Revolution," *Transactions of the New York Academy of Sciences*, Series II, No. 28, 73-80.
―――, 1967, *A Serbian Village: Social and Cultural Change in a Yugoslav Community*. New York: Harper & Row (Harper Colophon Books).
Herr, Richard, 1971, *Spain*. Englewood Cliffs, New Jersey: Prentice Hall.
*Informe Sociológico Sobre la Situación Social de España, 1970*. Madrid: Editorial Euramérica, S.A.
Kenny, Michael, 1960, "Patterns of Patronage in Spain," *Anthropological Quarterly*, No. 33, 14-23.
―――, 1961, *A Spanish Tapestry: Town and Country in Castile*. New York: Harper & Row (Harper Colophon Books).
Leeds, Anthony, 1965, "Brazilian Careers and Social Structure: A Case History and Model," in *Contemporary Cultures and Societies of Latin America*, ed. by Dwight W. Heath and Richard N. Adams. New York: Random House.

Mintz, Jerome R., 1972, "Trouble in Andalusia," *Natural History*, Vol. LXXXI, No. 5, 54-62.

Norbeck, Edward, 1966, *Changing Japan* (Case Study in Cultural Anthropology). New York: Holt, Rinehart and Winston.

Pelto, Pertti, 1970, *Anthropological Research: The Structure of Inquiry*. New York: Harper & Row.

Pitt-Rivers, Julian A., 1954, *The People of the Sierra*. Chicago: Chicago University Press (Phoenix books).

*Primer Censo Agrario de España, Año 1962, Huesca 22*. Madrid: Instituto Nacional de Estadística.

Roman, Manuel, 1971, *The Limits of Economic Growth in Spain*. New York: Praeger.

Silverman, Sydel F., 1965, "The Community-Nation Mediator in Traditional Central Italy," *Ethnology*, Vol. IV, No. 2, 172-189.

——, 1966, "An Ethnographic Approach to Social Stratification: Prestige in a Central Italian Community," *American Anthropologist*, Vol. 68, No. 4, 899-921.

Stirling, Paul, 1965, *Turkish Village*. New York: Wiley (Science editions).

Wolf, Eric R., 1956, "Aspects of Group Relations in a Complex Society: Mexico," *American Anthropologist*, Vol. 58, No. 6, 1065-1078.

——, 1966, "Kinship, Friendship, and Patron-Client Relations in Complex Societies," in *The Social Anthropology of Complex Societies*, ed. by Michael Banton. London: Tavistock Publications.

# Recommended reading

Aceves, Joseph, 1971, *Social Change in a Spanish Village.* Cambridge, Mass.: Schenkman Publishing Co.
    A study of a Castilian village in the province of Segovia. There is less about change, and more about cultural values, than the title would indicate.

Anlló-Vázquez, Juan, 1966, *Estructura y Problemas del Campo Español.* Madrid: Editorial Cuadernos para el Diálogo.
    A good overall survey of the transformation taking place in the Spanish countryside.

Banfield, Edward C., 1958, *The Moral Basis of a Backward Society.* New York: Free Press.
    A book about a southern Italian village which has stimulated a great deal of controversy in anthropology. The author believes a set of values, called "amoral familism" impede economic progress.

Bock, Philip K. (ed.), 1969, *Peasants in the Modern World.* Albuquerque: University of New Mexico Press.
    A collection of essays which deal with changing peasant societies in various areas of the world.

Brenan, Gerald, 1943, *The Spanish Labyrinth: An Account of the Social and Political Background of the Spanish Civil War.* Cambridge: Cambridge University Press (2d ed., 1950).
    An indispensable guide to Spanish society and history. It ranks among the finest books in English on Spain.

Carr, Raymond, 1966, *Spain: 1808-1939.* Oxford: Oxford University Press.
    A detailed, interpretive history of modern Spain which focuses on the Spanish attempt to create representative political institutions. As the title indicates, the book does not deal with events after the Civil War.

Foster, George M., 1967, *Tzintzuntzan: Mexican Peasants in a Changing World.* Boston: Little, Brown.
    A good monograph on a peasant community in Mexico. It contains certain theoretical frameworks which can be applied to peasant communities elsewhere.

Friedl, Ernestine, 1965, *Vasilika: A Village in Modern Greece* (Case Study in Cultural Anthropology). New York: Holt, Rinehart and Winston.
    A very readable account of a small village in Greece. There are many analogues to communities in Spain.

Herr, Richard, 1971, *Spain.* Englewood Cliffs: Prentice Hall.
    This is a short but good introduction to Spanish history by a noted historian. Especially interesting are the chapters on the post Civil War period.

Kenny, Michael, 1961, *A Spanish Tapestry: Town and Country in Castile.* New York: Harper & Row.
    The book is divided into two parts: the first is a study of a mountain village in Soria; the latter is of a parish in Madrid.

Lisón-Tolesano, Carmelo, 1966, *Belmonte de los Caballeros: A Sociological Study of a Spanish Town*. Oxford: Oxford University Press.
A study by a Spanish social anthropologist of his native village. Whereas many anthropologists have described Spanish communities as fundamentally egalitarian, Lison finds hierarchy and stratification to be important principles of community life.
Lopreato, Joseph, 1967, *Peasants No More: Social Class and Social Change in an Underdeveloped Society*. San Francisco: Chandler Publishing Co.
A study of southern Italian society which places special emphasis on the social consequences of emigration.
Michener, James A., 1968, *Iberia: Spanish Travels and Reflections*. New York: Random House.
A romantic account of contemporary Spain by a perceptive American novelist.
Pérez-Díaz, Víctor, 1966, *Estructura Social del Campo y Exodo Rural: Estudio de un Pueblo de Castila*. Madrid: Editorial Tecnos, S.A.
A brief study of a small community in Castile by a Spanish rural sociologist.
Pitt-Rivers, Julian A., 1954, *The People of the Sierra*. Chicago: University of Chicago Press.
This has been the most influential book by an anthropologist on Spain. It deals with a mountain village in Andalusia and describes some of the central values of Andalusian society.
Thomas, Hugh, 1961, *The Spanish Civil War*. New York: Harper & Row.
A readable and accurate account of the Civil War. The author has made a genuine effort to remain objective.
Wylie, Laurence, 1957, *Village in the Vaucluse: An Account of Life in a French Village*. New York: Harper & Row.
A delightful portrayal of the people of a small village in southern France.